BROKEN PAST
HEALS DREAMS

An Australian story of abuse, adversity and acceptance.

Joileen Mischel

Broken Past Heals Dreams: An Australian story of abuse, adversity and acceptance
© Joileen Mischel 2020

ISBN: 978-1-925935-86-8 (Paperback)
        978-1-925935-87-5 (eBook)

 A catalogue record for this book is available from the National Library of Australia

Editors: Peta Culverhouse and Beverley Streater
Cover Design: Ocean Reeve Publishing
Design and Typeset: Ocean Reeve Publishing
Printed in Australia by Ocean Reeve Publishing

Published by Joileen Mischel and Ocean Reeve Publishing
www.oceanreevepublishing.com

REEVE
PUBLISHING

Contents

Acknowledgments

There are a number people I feel compelled to acknowledge for the support, encouragement and love they gifted me throughout my life's journey. And more recently during the process of writing my story. During the writing process, while deeply reflecting on my life experiences, I realised there were many people along the way who, but for them, my life may have turned out very differently indeed. Many, who I have not acknowledged during my writing, have passed on; hopefully, I was able to successfully convey my gratitude for their support when I needed it most.

My special heartfelt love and gratitude must go to Sue, my dearest and most steadfast friend of more than 50 years. She has always been there during the significant periods of my life, and continues offering moral support and love. Sue has shown me that true friendship is commitment and loyalty above all else.

To my former partner Ron, I'm truly grateful for his support and ongoing encouragement and belief in my ability. I hope he realises how grateful I feel for his support during my health setbacks during the later years of our union. And also, my heartfelt thanks for his commitment to reading the first draft of my manuscript and continually encouraging me to keep at it.

I have immense gratitude for universal wisdom in gifting me with three unique children who fill my heart with pride as I recognise the wonderful adults they have become. Thanks too for their belief in my strength and courage during my many life challenges and their encouragement during the writing process. They and the grandchildren they have gifted me make my life truly worthwhile.

A heartfelt thankfulness must also go to my wonderful friend Fiona who has hung in there for the past twenty-five years, and encouraging me to keep writing, confident I would complete it. Thank you also to my dear friend Lyn for keeping me good humouredly positive and focused in some of the not so funny situations in recent years.

Another special friend Donna Maree, many thanks for encouraging me during some of my more recent challenges. Especially for cheering me on when I wondered if it was worth the effort required to complete it. You have been a great friend who always believed I could do it.

Finally, a big heartfelt thank you must go to Ocean Reeve (Superman) and Jason Smith (Flash) at Ocean Reeve Publishing. Each one continuously encouraged me to believe in myself and keep the faith in my ability to complete the task. I know I couldn't have managed to work through the intricacies of getting a manuscript to an actual book without their wisdom and support. Thanks Ocean and Jason for allowing me to work at my own pace without the pressure of a deadline.

Introduction

'Once you realise that the road is the goal and that you are always on the road, not to reach the goal, but to enjoy its beauty and its wisdom, life ceases to be a task and becomes natural and simple, in itself an ecstasy.'

— SRI NISARGADATTA MAHARAJ

Who doesn't love a good story. Especially stories about people who have learned from and transcended the trials that life has thrown at them. This story is about such a journey, on a path littered with many diverse and challenging experiences. As I contemplated the task ahead, there were times when I thought writing about them might be too difficult. Yet, my journey has defined me; from a place of displacement, sexual abuse, confusion of identity, to one of self-acceptance. I'm grateful for the journey and what I've learned along the way. I'm even more grateful for my ability to stay strong when I needed to, and to never lose sight of my dreams.

I tell my story, in order to inspire, motivate and encourage others to never give up on their dreams. I've learned that life is about personal experiences and choices and continually believing there is a purpose to it all. I realised long ago if I could jump the hurdles that were on my path—to not give in when things seemed almost unbearable—I could make my own dreams: completing my education; having children to love; traveling to far off places; having a worthwhile career where I could be of service to others, and to find out who I really was, come true.

Three score years and ten and counting. Am I there yet? Yes, miraculously, I've reached that milestone. The years have rolled along so effortlessly, well, maybe not so effortlessly, while I've faced my share of adversity and joy. What motivated me to hang on during those early years steeped in abuse, shame and fear? Certainly not because I felt loved or cherished. There were times when I felt almost desperately unloved and unlovable.

On reflection, I recognised I'd been gifted an innate form of strength, courage, optimism, and an intense determination to survive those early years of abusive. I was meant to survive—and I believed I could. I'm not sure what my optimism was based on; perhaps it was just innocent naivety. Or it might simply have been a subconscious inner knowing that kept me believing all would be well in the end.

Over the years, I lost count of the times my father uttered these terrifying words: 'You can't tell anyone about this. If you do, I'll get a gun and blow your head off, then I'll blow mine off, too.'

Even while enduring far too many years of sexual abuse, I didn't feel like a victim. Hiding from the fear and shame of it was just a normal part of my life. I simply accepted that if I could keep believing, someday it would be over.

My father's threats played into my childhood fear of dying. Even though I had no negative experience or understanding of death, I just knew I didn't want to die. It wasn't so much that I feared death, I simply couldn't grasp the idea I was here now, but one day I'd no longer 'be here.' Because of this inner fear, I did believe if I told anyone about what was happening, Dad would kill me! It's almost a lifetime ago, yet I can recall—like it was yesterday—the fear that inhabited my 'child mind.'

Over the years, the same questions arose: *After I die, will I remember any of this? Why am I living this experience to one day no longer be here?* I don't want to live forever, yet neither do I want to one day pass into nothingness; to no longer exist. I've forged a successful and happy life. Yet, being human, those troubling thoughts have occasionally resurfaced, that small child still lurked somewhere at a subconscious level.

My search for answers has been enduring. At times, I've felt like I've been living in suspended animation, waiting for something to happen. What? I simply don't know. As the years moved slowly forward, there was always that feeling of 'How much longer?', 'When will my life journey end?', 'Is planning ahead really worth the effort?' 'Is there a purpose to it all?'

That's when my rational mind rears up and I think, *Yes there is a purpose!* I've realised it's not for me to search for the purpose but to merely let life unfold as it will, to accept that I am on an individual journey of discovery. Fortunately, because of my spiritual quest, I've gained wisdom, and a greater understanding of life's purpose, which has enabled me to alleviate many of those childhood fears.

While I haven't always been able to anticipate the obstacles ahead, I made a choice long ago to not let my past difficulties define or destroy me. Even so, I confess there have been times when I've found it difficult to stop focusing on my shortcomings; to not compare my life with another's. Times when I've felt my own achievements haven't measured up; not wanting to accept second best. Coming to terms with and accepting who I am is perhaps one of the biggest challenges I've faced.

My ongoing spiritual quest has helped me slay many of those demons. I've come to understand that life is something we have chosen, not something that happened to us. While I have no idea why we have embarked upon it, I've come to believe we are all a part of some grand mysterious plan of which we are a minute but important part. It could simply be that, as some would have it, we are here merely by complete and utter chance, with no higher purpose than the simple life of a sand fly. Nonetheless, I have learned one important thing: while life can throw up some tricky and sometimes seemingly impossible challenges, we can choose how to respond to them. It's about acceptance and a sense of mindfulness.

I offer this story with gratitude. Although I have no religious allegiance, I can look back and acknowledge God's hand at my elbow. The many times when I'd felt lost and alone, wondering how I'd go on, His angels held my hands and guided me. My hope is that my story will in some way inspire and encourage others to persevere in their own quest—to draw strength from the well deep within—and like I have done, to never lose sight of their dreams.

Part 1

*'You're braver than you believe, and stronger than you seem,
and smarter than you think.'*

— CHRISTOPHER ROBIN (WINNIE THE POOH)

Chapter 1

Where And How Did It All Begin?

'Thank Christ you're not mine!'

When my father flung these cruel words at me—words that changed my life forever—I was fourteen years old. I'd already endured ten years of sexual abuse, so to hear him tell me I was adopted, that he wasn't my father, was both a shock and an enormous relief. After all the years he'd taunted me saying, 'I know something about you that I can't tell you,' here it was—I was adopted. Realising his immoral blood wasn't running through my veins was a great revelation. Knowing this, however, only made Mum's ongoing taunts 'You're just like your father,' even more hurtful.

That was sixty years ago! I realise now the resilience I developed in those painful years was what I was able to draw from in the many trials that lay ahead. Many of my life experiences, both joyful and sad, have been forgotten, because they didn't have much impact. This one, however, is indelibly imprinted on my memory. And unfortunately, it was one more secret I had to keep, another confirmation of rejection. This secret was the mystery of who I really was; a secret that would remain unsolved for another thirty-three years.

Who was that young girl? Where did it all begin? Children, I believe, are beautifully innocent lovers of life and I, of course, was no different. My earliest clear memory was at three years of age, a happy one of me and my four-year old cousin Trent, taking a plane trip alone, from Kingaroy to Brisbane, Queensland. What excitement we felt as the flight attendants fussed over us, offering minties and chocolates. Then my happiness turning to disappointment and unhappy tears when we arrived in Brisbane and I realised I'd left my beloved gollywog doll on the plane.

I hold special childhood memories of our Sunday visits to Nana who lived alone in her quintessential Queenslander house in Boondall, Brisbane. Her home, although simply furnished, was comfortable and welcoming. Highly-polished dark wood furniture created a feeling of warmth – and taking pride of place on the silky oak mantelpiece in the living room was Nana's impressive chiming clock. When staying overnight, I slept on the old-style settee in the living room. If I woke in the dark of night, I always felt comforted as I lay listening to the clock's rhythmic ticking and chiming on the quarter hour.

Just outside the kitchen, the backdoor opened to a long flight of wooden steps leading down into the large fenced backyard. From the top of the steps, one could look out on a vast expanse of farmland on the far side of the railway track, where herds of dairy cattle grazed – this area is now the Brisbane Entertainment Centre. A creaky wooden gate opened out on to a gravel laneway running alongside the busy railway line into the city. As the coal-fired trains departed from the station nearby, thick black smoke would belch high into the sky, descending as grainy soot which filtered through the open train windows to settle on the carriage seats.

Tucked away against the back fence, beside a handyman-constructed chook pen, the residence of a couple of happy hens, stood the antiquated wooden, outdoor dunny. An assortment of crawly creatures, including red-back spiders, happily set up home in the darkness. The atmosphere after dark was especially scary because the only visible light was a dim glow emanating from the top of the steps, or the beam of a small hand-held torch. At night we kids were always relieved to have someone standing on guard outside the dunny door.

For me, though, the highlight of our visits was watching Nana at her nightly ritual when I'd sit, fascinated, as she wound her long, fine, grey hair in pins before going to bed. The next morning, I'd watch entranced as she styled it into a bun at the nape of her neck. She did this, unfailingly, every day. Perhaps it was this fascination that gave Mum the impression I wanted to be a hairdresser.

Not prone to idle chatter and gossip, Nana was a kindly-spoken lady who emanated a quiet, calm presence. She was always neat and well-presented. And I don't remember her ever raising her voice to any of her grandkids. Although she wasn't overly affectionate, I knew Nana loved me, and I dearly loved her in return. Sunday lunch always included home-made ice-cream, and red jelly made especially for me.

During school holidays, I often spent a few days at Nana's by myself. Sunday was church day; Nana wore a full-length body corset under her best dark-blue suit. As she stood holding on to the bed frame, I'd help tighten the corset laces. This intrigued me; I'd wonder why she went to so much trouble just to go to church. But she did look very smart and I always felt so proud to be introduced as her granddaughter. On our return home, she'd head to her bedroom saying she was tired and needed forty winks; a few minutes of nap time to recharge her batteries.

My cousin, Trent, and his family lived around the corner and we'd play for hours with the neighbourhood kids out the front of Nana's house, looking for tadpoles after it rained. Or we'd fish for yabbies in the gutters full of muddy water, by dropping a string fishing line with a bit of meat tied on the end into a hole in the gutter where the yabbies lived. Any success was always followed by shouts of triumph. Those were the days of innocence, the good memories of so long ago.

When I had my own children, I recalled these and many other lovely childhood memories. Watching my children play for hours in the bush out the back of our house and riding their bikes to and from school, brought back fond recollections of me and my brother Wayne, who was three years younger than me, walking barefoot to and from school. My older son Craig once commented that he'd had a great early childhood and it filled me with a sense of satisfaction. I thought—having fulfilled one of my earliest dreams to be a mother—maybe I got some of it right after all.

For a number of years, when I drove to Brisbane from my former home on the Sunshine Coast in Queensland, I'd take a tour past Nana's old home for a boost of nostalgia – taking the opportunity to reminiscence on those happy times. It's gratifying to know that in this modern world of knocking down and rebuilding, Nana's house still stands as majestically as it ever did, although now painted a bright shade of terracotta.

Chapter 2

My Parents

Naturally, like most children, I just accepted Mum and Dad as they were. It was only later, as I reached my teens, that I began to wonder what attracted them to each other; because by temperament and environment, they were two very different people.

My Father

Albert, or Bert, as Dad was commonly called, came from Bundaberg, Queensland. He was the youngest of seven children born to German parents. Only he and his brother Emil, one year his senior, were born in Australia after their parents immigrated. Grandma, Dad's mother, who I remember as being short and plump, was a pleasant yet reserved woman who spoke poor heavily-accented English. And although communication was difficult, I remember her as a kindly lady who smiled often.

Unfortunately, Grandma developed gangrene in her feet as the result of age-related diabetes. My last memory of her was when I was about ten years old, visiting her in hospital after she'd had foot surgery. She passed away not long after. I know nothing of what became of Dad's father. I have only vague recollections of his step-father Max, also a German immigrant, who I remember as being a very short, solemn man. Since he also spoke rather poor English, trying to have a normal conversation with him was almost impossible, thus I never got to know him well.

Dad was tall and lanky, with fine, wispy, dark hair, cruel thin lips, and small dark brown deep-set eyes which could bore a hole into my young soul. He was, in fact, a man who never outwardly displayed any softness in his character. He was one who oozed sinister humour. Impatient and intimidating, he'd explode with anger when things didn't go his way. For someone well over six feet, he had noticeably small hands and feet. His hands were calloused and hard, his short, ugly fingers stained orange by nicotine. He took great joy in making sure my brother Wayne and I were often on the receiving end of those hands. And if by chance he missed, he'd lash out with his foot.

Apart from the physical abuse he metered out, Dad's ridiculing words and derogatory comments could cut to the core, eradicating any self-esteem we might have had. He'd simply laugh at our discomfort – if we cried he'd taunt us, promising 'more of the same.' A boastful and shocking liar, his only friends over the years were his fishing mates, avid card players, or other deviates as we were to later realise. We rarely had visitors to our home. Wayne and I eventually realised Dad wasn't particularly liked or respected by other adults.

My Mother

Mum, Gwendoline or Gwen, as she was called, was a country girl, the elder of two sisters who grew up on a dairy farm in the Nanango district of Queensland. She was a petite five-foot two-inches tall, feminine and softly spoken, and until later in life, finely built. She had small, hazel grey eyes and a clear, almost alabaster, English rose complexion which she retained until the end of her life. She took great care of her skin and always wore lipstick. Unlike her mother who had always kept her hair long, Mum wore her fine mousy, brown hair, cut short and permed. My early memories of her were of a sweet woman with a gentle smile who was always kind to people in need.

Growing up, Mum benefited from many of the same opportunities as most young women of the day: a good education; cooking and sewing lessons; and piano tutoring to the extent of her teacher's ability. Her extended family also lived and farmed in the Nanango area and followed a strict Methodist religion; her father being a lay preacher in their local church. The religious constraints on her social activities though were rather severe; the local dances – where young men and women had close physical contact – were seen as an unacceptable activity for young women. Modern music and dancing would, according to her father, contradict their religious teachings of discouraging close physical contact between young men and unmarried women.

Having had no sons, Mum's father treated her as his right-hand man and taught her everything about running a dairy farm. She reportedly loved it although she regularly told us how hard she had worked during those dairy farming years. She was also a competent horsewoman in her youth.

Mum and Dad were married in 1940, both twenty-seven years old. It was an era where people believed if a woman was still unmarried in her late twenties, she was considered 'an old maid'. Mum, perhaps believing she was at risk of being left on the shelf—a common reference—chose a man whose upbringing was entirely at odds with her own. The attraction may have been that he was tall, slim and at that time very good looking, or it could simply have been that she was genuinely in love with him.

Dad, a cold, unfeeling excuse for a man, became increasingly emotionally and psychologically cruel as the years passed – ridiculing almost everything Mum did. It's astounding how quickly he succeeded in eroding her self-confidence. By the time she understood what was happening, it was too late; I doubt she even realised what was going on. Gradually, over the years, his continual citing of safety issues, meant that by the time I was eight years old she no longer drove the car.

Eventually, when I was 23 years old, and only four years after I'd left home, Dad, after having had many illicit liaisons, abandoned Mum for another woman. While I may not have been aware of it at the time, I think witnessing Mum's submission to Dad's conduct over the years saw me unconsciously develop a deep-seated aversion to marriage.

Chapter 3

Where Was Our Hometown?

Where are you from, or where's your hometown? A common question most people ask. I'd love to say, 'My hometown is …,' but unfortunately, I don't have one. Because Dad was an unskilled labourer, he moved us from place to place in his never-ending search for work. In fact, looking back, almost all my formative years were spent moving from one town to the next. The nomadic lifestyle of constantly saying goodbye and moving on was one which continued well into my adulthood.

Would my early life have been happier if I'd grow up in the one house in one town making memories with special friends during those formative years? Who knows. Perhaps it might have been if the sexual abuse had not been a large part of my life. One unfortunate consequence of this itinerant lifestyle was that I formed no special attachments to anyone or anything during those early years.

I have clear memories of Dad cutting sugar cane in North Queensland. The cane would be burned in the evening, and cut by hand the following day using a special machete style cane knife. There was always multitudes of raging fires scattered throughout the cane farming district, burning well into the night. It was an amazing sight for us kids to watch, as the bright, red-hot flames licked gloriously high into the night sky. It was a hard life for the cane cutters and their families though, as the accommodation provided by the cane farmers was rudimentary; a basic wooden two room hut with poor ventilation and a wood stove which functioned as heater in the colder months and kept the hut hellishly hot in the summer months. I remember clearly, after a long day in the cane field, Dad would return to our hut at dusk, covered in black soot with only his eyes visible, ready to slip into the metal bathtub in front of the wood stove.

After the cane season wound up, our family spent the next six months as part of a travelling carnival. Mum enjoyed travelling and the social aspect of it, but she found carnival life was a difficult lifestyle to maintain with two young children. I was five years old at the time, and recall going to a huge number of different schools, some for only a few days—one for only half a day. What a surprise I got when Mum came to pick me up at lunch time that day!

During those early years, Mum demonstrated how competent and confident a woman she was. I vividly recall one occasion when we were travelling with the carnival, where, without hesitation, she drove our Model T Ford car through a dangerously flooded creek to reach the next town in time to set up for the carnival. To me, my mother could do almost anything, and I was so proud of her. However, by the time I was ten years old, my mother's self-confidence had been totally eroded; her former skills and interests ceased to exist.

After leaving the carnival, we moved further out into Western Queensland, where Dad was employed. His main task constructing fences on a sheep and cattle station. These outback stations covered vast expanses of land and controlling the movement of the stock over such an area was difficult; thus the construction of extensive boundary fencing was critical. It took many months for the workers, or fencers as they were called, to construct the kilometres of fencing across thousands of hectares.

The outback was a harsh, unforgiving environment; the land was dry and parched, and rain deprived for most of the year. Surface water was unavailable, so drinking water for the animals was drawn up by bores drilled into the artesian basin flowing deep below the surface of the land. The water pumped up or drawn up by windmills was generally boiling hot when it reached the surface. The water was then directed into the many bore drains, or channels, which had been dug throughout the properties; sometimes these drains extended for kilometres crisscrossing many stations.

Our living standards were very basic; some might think rather rough and ready. Our campsite consisted of two basic railway tents erected under the few gum trees growing close to the bore drain. One tent was allocated as our sleeping quarters, another was set up as a kitchen/dining area. While the tall gum trees surrounding our camp gave very little worthwhile protection from the extreme heat, it was better than nothing. Mum had the ultimate privilege of cooking on a primitive wood-fired stove situated in one corner of the tent.

Perishable food, which needed to be kept cool, was stored in a Coolgardie safe—an Australian food storage unit invented during the gold rush period of the late 19th century. It hung in the shade of a tree which aided in keeping the contents cool and prolong the life of the food kept inside it. Our drinking water was carted in drums or barrels from the station homestead water tanks. Canvas water bottles filled with our drinking water were hung in the shade of a tree, waiting for a cool breeze.

Shopping for our foodstuffs and basic necessities was mostly done by the property owners' wife, who regularly drove into the nearest township a few hours away. Often though, a transport driver who delivered equipment to the surrounding stations would collect our list of requirements and deliver them to us on his next trip out.

It was a hot, arid country, totally lacking in humidity. During summer, the intense heat of the sun baked the earth to a dry ochre. The long grass, which grew to over 150 centimeters during the winter months, would be scorched to a burnished copper by the harsh summer sun. We kids never ventured far from the campsite for fear of becoming lost in the long grass or possibly falling into a bore drain. No doubt Mum found living under such harsh conditions difficult, with much of her day taken up with the routine chores of camp life, and caring for a continual stream of orphaned animals.

To supplement his fencing income, Dad spent his spare time shooting kangaroos – deemed a pest by pastoralists – for their hides. The kangaroo hides were very popular at the time as floor matting or wall hangings. It was normal for the parched earth surrounding our campsite to be swept smooth and covered with dozens of kangaroo hides nailed out to dry, after being meticulously prepared by rubbing salt on the inside of the skin to dry off the surplus flesh. The big red kangaroos, although quite rare, were magnificent in size and colour and were particularly sought after. A contractor called on a regular basis to collect the hides from the various kangaroo shooters scattered throughout Western Queensland.

Chapter 4

Home Schooling Before Moving On

My first experience of home schooling was as a five-year-old, sitting in our tent with Mum teaching me lessons sent through the Queensland Correspondence School. I loved the schoolwork; it was always exciting to receive an envelope containing my new lessons.

Our spare time, which for us kids was plentiful, was spent helping Mum with the orphaned baby animals who needed special care. The lambs were orphaned when their mothers became bogged and perished in the bore drains, where they went seeking drinking water. Their need for water was understandable, but unfortunately, when the water was low, the drain became a bog, which meant the sides were then too steep and muddy for the ewe to scramble out. Even as many were successfully pulled free of the mud, many others would simply give up and refuse to be rescued. Still others, after being rescued, would soon enough return to the drains and inevitable death.

Those that became stranded in the bog were fair prey for the predatory crow. As soon as an animal became helpless, the crows, just watching and waiting for such an occasion, would swoop to pick out their eyes. Once the crow did its deed, the ewe would inevitably perish where she was bogged. As children living on the land, Wayne and I learned and accepted that this was just nature's way. This sad event meant the ewe's lamb was left motherless. Whilst in our care, many lambs would make their home in a box by the wood stove in our tent. We'd continue bottle feeding these babies with a special formula until they were old enough and strong enough to return to the flock.

The death of female kangaroos killed by the shooters also often left their joeys motherless, an orphan unable to fend for itself. Typically, a joey stays in its mother's pouch till around six months of age, which meant when the mother roo was shot, the joey would be bought back to our tent for Mum to care for. A makeshift hessian pouch— resembling the mother's pouch—would be their home until they had grown bigger. Like the lambs, the kangaroo joey was a loveable little animal which quickly won our hearts. Naturally, we made pets of these animals and felt sad when it was time to release them back into their own natural habitat.

As young children, life didn't present many negatives; we were resilient and just accepted life as it came. Yet, bad things can happen when you least expect it. An unfortunately distressing event that year is certainly memorable. The height of summer usually brought with it the threat of fires and the property owners, 'cockies' as they were called, kept a close eye on their stock so they could be moved quickly if needed. One extremely hot and cloudless day, without warning, a hot westerly wind suddenly developed, and in wild abandon, raced across the countryside blowing the long, dry grass sideways. Then, seemingly out of nowhere, a raging fire, driven onward by the wind, rampaged across the landscape. Fanned by the hot airstream the fire ate everything in its path, forcing the animals to run and take cover wherever they could.

Unfortunately, the new fences—erected to keep the animals' safe— ultimately led many to their sad demise. While attempting to escape the terrible inferno, many hundreds of sheep and cattle became trapped and perished while huddled together in the corners of the newly fenced paddocks. The surviving sheep were almost unrecognisable; the wool on their bodies charred black by the fire. To be a child witnessing such devastation was extremely heart-breaking. Later, as we drove around the property counting the dead animals and surveying the devastation, we realised how lucky we were to have escaped.

The only good news that day was that the station owners prize bull was later found bogged in one of the bore drains where it had no doubt sought shelter. The devastation of the many animals was temporarily put aside. The bulls rescue became a major undertaking which took many men, with the assistance of a tractor, many hours to finally extract it from the muddy bore drain.

The fire and resulting death rate of the animals had unfortunate consequences for our family. The result of many months of intense work constructing the fences had been destroyed. The loss of livestock and property infrastructure also meant the station owners could no longer afford to employ permanent workers. Once more we were uprooted as Dad began searching further afield for employment.

Luck prevailed, and Dad secured a job working on the Jack Taylor Weir, being built on the Balonne River at St George in the inland region of Southern Queensland. We were even further out west now—approximately 500 kilometres from the east coast. Mum was employed as a camp cook for the workers in the construction camp. It was not long after WW II when home-grown workers were in short supply and Australia began accepting immigrants from Europe. The camp community consisted of a mix of Australian workers and European men from the Baltic countries of Latvia, Lithuania, and Estonia. They were commonly referred to as Balts.

Still only five years old, and with correspondence lessons behind me, I was enrolled at the St George Primary School where I attended for six months. Because I'd previously attended so many schools, I felt happy thinking we would be staying for a little longer. After school, I'd spend time in the hot kitchen with Mum while she prepared the men's evening meal. I'd help out by setting and putting the butter out on the tables; it always fascinated me how quickly the butter turned to oil.

Luckily for mum, Wayne was a good-natured little kid who spent the long day in the hot kitchen with her. He'd sit in the kitchen, in a big washtub filled with water to keep him cool while she worked; no doubt he probably thought it was great fun. The men thought he was handsome, and always commented on how big he was for a two-year-old. Eventually, as with all jobs, the project at St George eventually came to an end and it was then that we returned to live in Brisbane. And it was here, during the following four years, that my life as I knew it would slowly change in a most disturbing way.

Chapter 5

School Years

Yes, I'm grateful for those early years and the many childhood memories that I've retained. Reflecting on the person I've become, it is obvious that much of who I am now can be attributed to those happier times. Growing up physically active, running barefoot and free, and going to school without a compulsory uniform was freedom. I can't remember worrying about what I wore to school; for me, it was more about learning and playing a sport. And no school shoes, just sandals, discarded by little lunch and put back on to walk home. I'm sure witnessing Mum's resilience under trying circumstances in those early years was stored in my subconscious memory.

Unlike Wayne, who was a head above other kids his age, I was small, and I looked a lot younger than I was. My Grade five class photograph, where we were all lined up along the length of a building shows me as the second shortest in a class of forty-four. Yes, that was the average class size back then. Being small never bothered me, though. What I lost in size I made up for in speed.

I was a tomboy. I had no interest in sitting under the trees talking girl-talk. I preferred playing with boys—not talking about them—mainly because some of them could run faster than me and I absolutely loved the challenge and the competition. We couldn't wait to play red rover at lunchtime, and if we hadn't been made to sit and eat lunch, I'm sure we wouldn't have bothered eating at all. Being the fastest girl at school, which in those days went to Grade eight, had prestige. Although I lacked self-confidence in many other areas, I made up for it on the field and enjoyed the admiration that being a good athlete gained.

Unlike many of my friends, I hated missing school; I was too afraid I'd miss out on something. I wasn't a genius by any stretch of the imagination but I did my best and usually managed to be among the few top students in my class. The class was graded, and everyone knew where they were ranked because we were seated—as sad as it now seems—accordingly, from top to bottom. It certainly created a competitive atmosphere. For those of us who didn't want to be outside the top few places, it was the reason to work just that little bit harder.

Wayne wasn't as capable a student as I was. He was a lovely, sensitive, little chap who'd always been big for his age, and unfortunately, being bigger wasn't necessarily better. It was in many ways a disadvantage as many adults and teachers had unrealistic expectations of him because of his size – they made no allowances for his lack of emotional and intellectual maturity and development.

There have always been people who should've known better, who lack awareness of how a few thoughtless words can impact a vulnerable child. I remember my sixth-grade teacher, the school principal no less, bringing Wayne into my classroom and asking him why he couldn't be more like his sister. I felt sad and embarrassed to see Wayne shamed in front of my classmates. I knew he had qualities I didn't have; he was more than three years my junior, yet his oral reading skills were far superior to mine. Regrettably, our itinerant lifestyle meant Wayne's education, like mine, was left incomplete; he was forced to leave school midway through Grade five. It was only his ability to read well that enabled him to educate himself somewhat in the ensuing years.

While I loved reading and devoured the school library books daily, I was terrified of reading in front of my class. When I was unfortunate enough to be nominated to read, my voice would quiver and my hand holding the book would sweat and shake while I held back tears of embarrassment. My Grade six class was regularly asked to bring a newspaper clipping to read in class, but Dad absolutely forbade me reading anything in a newspaper.

Having to explain that to an unbelieving teacher was difficult and I'm sure he had doubts about many of my excuses. Dad's contradictory and intimidating ways were at times hard to fathom and so I found it hard to know what he really believed. One part of him seemed to be keeping me innocent of the world and what was happening while another part was taking and abusing that innocence.

Chapter 6

The Secret I Had To Keep

My earliest memories of sexual abuse were as a four-year-old whilst living in Hervey Bay, Queensland; then later when we'd moved out to western Queensland. At that age, it wasn't frightening because I was too young to understand what was happening. It was just a secret, one that even then I never felt comfortable keeping. I clearly remember an incident when Dad was on the fencing job. We went to the property owners for a visit, and the young children wanted me to play mothers and fathers; show me yours and I'll show you mine sort of game, but I just couldn't join in. I'm sure it was because of what I was experiencing with Dad; a part of me felt uneasy even at that age.

It was after we moved back to Brisbane when I was six years old that the clear and disturbing incidences became more real. In the beginning it was only Sunday mornings before going to Sunday School, while Mum was preparing breakfast. Dad would call me to his bed for a 'cuddle' which was how he described rubbing his penis at the entrance to my vagina. He always said it was a secret, and if anyone found out he would go to jail. I was too young to be keeping such secrets. I hated this Sunday morning ritual and I'd try to hide away. When Mum found me, I'd say I didn't want to go in, but he'd be calling, and she'd always insist I go in.

Our home at that time consisted of a three-room building, formally an army demountable, with a bathroom/laundry attachment at the back. The three rooms were merely a bedroom, a lounge room and a kitchen. An outdoor toilet, common at the time, was situated midway down the backyard. A wood copper, used for heating water or the weekly washing, was set up permanently, not far from the laundry door. On washing day, Mum would light the fire and boil the whites. Our washing line consisted of two long wires strung up between two poles across the yard propped up in the middle by a pole to support the weight of the washing.

The big backyard comfortably housed a couple of chicken and duck pens. We regularly had new batches of chickens and ducklings, which we raised and then dressed for sale. I really loved them and always felt sad when they grew up to be killed and eaten. The ducks were housed separately in a specially-designed fenced-off run, which had a shallow water pond. I don't remember feeling squeamish when the heads were chopped off, it just seemed a natural part of life. By the time I was nine years old, I was plucking and gutting the birds with Dad. My conscientious work ethic, I imagine, started back then.

Wayne and I slept in a big double bed in the middle room, which also doubled as the lounge room. The room was sparsely decorated except for Mum's treadle sewing machine and the large round-faced cabinet that housed the wireless. My love of a well-told story originated back then while listening to the Wednesday and Sunday night *Playhouse* plays on the wireless. I'd lie in bed wide awake, entranced, listening to a story, hoping desperately it wouldn't be in two episodes, which meant I'd have to wait another week for the conclusion. The anticipation of what would happen next was exciting, imagining all kinds of scenarios to bring the story to a close.

I'm convinced these stories, many of which were way above my understanding, trained me to use my imagination. Perhaps this is why I now thoroughly enjoy listening to the audiobooks when I travel in my car. I have access to other worlds where imagination can have its way.

Loving stories as I did during those early school years, I was never without a book to read. Later, while working in the fields, I always had a book stuck in the back pocket of my jeans, so I could snatch a short read at break time. During my teens, books were my escape, my retreat into another world away from the work and the sexual abuse. Reading kept me from thinking about what awaited me in the night or what work was ahead of me tomorrow.

Being settled didn't mean I no longer changed schools. During the next four years, I attended five schools, one for only a week while staying with my cousin Trent and his family on the other side of the city. The final school was for two years when Wayne started school, and I was in Grades four and five, and it was convenient for us to walk to school.

Our school had a tennis court and many of the students spent their lunch break practicing for the Friday afternoon sports competition. Dad and Mum had often spoken of how they'd enjoyed playing tennis in their youth; Dad still had a couple of his racquets at home. When I asked if I could play on sports afternoon at school he refused outright, and there was never an explanation why. Dad never gave reasons why. Looking back, I can see it was the beginning of Dad's objective to control my life.

Living in suburbia certainly brought with it many lifestyle adjustments. Until milk started being delivered in bottles, the daily horse-drawn milk cart would come down the street and we'd run down to the gate with our billycan to buy our daily quota. The baker, arriving in his horse-drawn cart, also came to the door with many varieties of bread in a wicker basket hooked over his arm; the deliciously fragrant aroma wafting off the bread as he ran up to the door. The fruit truck loaded with fresh produce would come twice a week and the ladies would all congregate at its side, ready to buy the choicest of fruit and vegetables. Then there was the soft drink truck, which slowly inched its way down the street every couple of weeks the driver ringing the bell, followed by the local kids. Before we purchased a refrigerator, we had an ice chest into which the ice man would place a large block of ice every few days.

Apart from Sundays, my life was like most kids in the area; school and playing in the yard after school. However, I don't remember being encouraged to have friends over to play when Dad was at home. In those early years, I have no recollection of ever having a birthday party either. Strange as it seems, when I was invited to a school friend's birthday party a few years later, I was absolutely scared stiff and simply didn't go. The first personal birthday I truly remember celebrating was my 50th.

Chapter 7

Goodbye Brisbane – A Journey South

O ur time living in Brisbane finally ended during the Christmas holiday period of 1955/56. Dad's wander lust, his continual need to move on, had gripped him again and after four years working at the local steel foundry, he quit. He'd heard that work was abundant in the southern states therefore our house was sold, replaced by a caravan, and plans made to head out on what he considered a new adventure.

However, the departure date of our southern journey was temporarily postponed due to Mums slow recovery from glandular fever. Fortunately, the new owners of our house kindly allowed us to park our caravan on the front lawn until Mum recovered enough to travel. We soon realised that living in a 12-foot caravan was to be a challenge for a family of four. There was no extra space for knickknacks or small treasures: only the very basic necessities of life. Wayne and I slept in the double bed at the back of the caravan while Mum and Dad collapsed the table down each night to make their bed.

After a number of weeks delay, we finally set off on our journey south in our lovely big black Buick car, towing our ugly, home-built, masonry caravan. By New Year we'd arrived at our destination, and were living, or more so camping, in the Stockton Caravan Park, a beach suburb across the Hunter River from Newcastle, New South Wales. Fortunately, within a few days of our arrival Dad had found employment at BHP Steel Works in Newcastle.

As luck would have it, even though we were living in a caravan park surrounded by other campers, Dad managed to continue my sexual abuse. The fact that I'd revealed to Mum, some weeks before we left Brisbane how he'd been regularly sexually abusing me, seemed not to deter him. I'd been having a vaginal discharge and was washing my briefs in the laundry when the new owner of our house noticed me and thought it was strange behaviour for a ten-year-old. She alerted Mum, who then, unbeknown to me, took my briefs to the doctor to see what the problem might be, only to be told someone had been sexually 'interfering' with me.

Later, when Mum asked me if I'd been meeting men on my way home from school, I had tearfully denied it. With her pressuring me, through sobs and fear of what might happen when dad found out, I told her it was Daddy. Now, here I was, walking along the beach with him, up behind the sand dunes, feeling terrified that someone would see us. I felt confused and let down; *Surely,* I thought, *after I'd told Mum what Dad had been doing to me, she'd be suspicious of him wanting to go off alone with me?* I felt utterly powerless. It was a bewildering and frightening time – I couldn't understand why Mum hadn't said anything more to me after my disclosure and her later talk with Dad. It was simply never discussed again and I just assumed she didn't believe me.

The school year arrived, and Wayne and I were enrolled in the Stockton Primary School; a totally alien environment compared to our Queensland school. Here, the school rules and dress regulations were very strict, a far cry from the barefoot and casual dress code we'd been used to. Now in Grade six, I was decked out in a formal day uniform during lesson times, and a sports uniform for physical education activities a few afternoons each week. No longer barefoot and carefree either, as we were always required to wear shoes.

The whole environment seemed foreign. I was surprised when the teachers insisted I change my writing style, but I eventually got the hang of it. The most surprising school rule though was not to be found in the classroom: it was in the playground. While the boys and girls were co-ed during lessons, out in the playground we were segregated. A fence was erected midway across the sports fields and the boys played on one side while the girls played on the other. Having come from an environment where most of my school breaks were spent playing and running with the boys, I was disappointed. However, despite the playground restrictions, I enjoyed the new school environment. I was an enquiring student who loved learning, so I caught on reasonably well. Even though I'd been at my previous school for two years, my earlier school experiences meant I still had feelings of insecurity. Perhaps, because I'd attended so many schools over the years, I just naturally held back from getting too attached to anything or anyone. There was always a sense of inevitability: this good time wouldn't last. As it happened, this was proven once again, when two months into the school term, Dad announced we were moving on. He had a new job working on the Hume Dam on the Murray River, on the New South Wales/Victorian border.

Experiencing new places and schools may seem exciting to some, but for me, the constant change compounded my feelings of sadness. I always found saying goodbye to my new friends distressing. Over the years, my emotional goodbyes became a standing joke within my family and the wider community. My inability to control my emotions has continually caused me extreme embarrassment during my lifetime. Over time, I learned the best way to avoid the pain and embarrassment was to not get too attached. Then I could simply walk away; no farewell parties; no goodbyes; no looking back—just leave. It wasn't until many years later, when I found my true birth history, that I finally understood the deep sense of loss I felt each time I said goodbye to someone I'd begun to care about.

Subsequently, this constant change and moving on hindered, to some degree, my ability to develop the skill of connecting and trusting others. I believe that subconsciously I held back, knowing any new relationship I developed would be temporary. The pain of losing that relationship would cause me more sadness and of course more embarrassment. It seemed easier to not allow myself to care.

Chapter 8

More Sad Goodbyes And Moving Ever Southward

And then it was over! Our ideal beachside living and new school experience had ended; the sad goodbyes to new friends were made, and we were once more on our southward journey. It was a leisurely, pleasant, and almost uneventful journey as we departed Stockton; a long trip which involved many days driving through unfamiliar territory. We'd almost reached our destination and looked forward to settling into our new surroundings when disaster struck. Dad had pulled off to the side of the road at the bottom of a steep gradient on the highway, to consult a roadmap. Gradually, we became aware of an ominous and unfamiliar deep-throated roar, which seemed to grow louder and bolder by the moment.

From out of nowhere, we were hit by what felt like an explosion, as the tail end of a semitrailer tore out the side of our caravan, leaving a gaping hole in its side, and scouring deep grooves down the side of our vehicle. The damage was immense. The cupboards busted and flung open to deposit all and sundry on to the caravan floor. Almost everything we owned had been broken or strewn throughout the interior, covered with a heavy layer of flour, sugar, clothing, and broken crockery.

Although, shocked and disorientated, we were grateful that none of us were harmed. After regaining our equilibrium, we were faced with the task of completing our journey towing a crippled and trashed caravan. Slowly, after making some minor adjustments and repairs, we were able to cautiously limp our way to our destination, eventually arriving late, but safe. Tired and relieved, we parked our caravan on the banks of the Murray River, at the bottom of the nearby Hume Dam.

By now, the crisp autumn weather was turning colder. Dad somehow managed to obtain some canvas sheeting to temporarily cover the caravan damage. However, it was many weeks before the outside damage was repaired enough for us to complete the internal repairs. We didn't have an annex attached to the caravan, which meant it was difficult storing the odds and ends we needed. As I reflect on that experience, I can only imagine how dreadful a period it must have been for Mum, having to deal with the horrific mess and utter chaos it created. In those early days, she wasn't one to complain, I just remember her taking it in her stride.

The area below the weir, where we had set up camp, was surprisingly lovely when we could finally appreciate it. Our caravan was situated under a gum tree, below the dam spillway, surrounded by lush green grass that grew right down to the water's edge. In the background, the water cascaded gently down the dam's massive concrete spillway to amble slowly and peacefully past our caravan site. Our lifestyle was ideal and we all loved it. It was here, on the riverbank, that I caught my first fish.

Most of the other male campsite occupants, who were set up around us, worked on the dam spillway construction with Dad, and I remember it being a very friendly little community. Once again, many of these men were European immigrants, like the men Dad had previously worked with in Queensland. The men who didn't live at the dam camping area lived in the Bonegilla Migrant Camp nearby.

Not long after arriving, I was befriended by a lovely European lady who was camped nearby. She was sweet-natured and kind, clearly well into her late forties. It's strange how certain experiences impacted my life, and how they've sat dormant in the back of my mind all these years. This lady, married to a much younger European man, told everyone she was thirty-nine years old. I recall feeling sorry that people were being unkind, and talking behind her back, joking about how she was trying to deceive people about her real age. I thought she was lovely as she spent a great deal of time with me, after school and on weekends, teaching me how to crochet. She was as proud of me as I was of myself when I was able to crochet colourful little teapot cosies. I'm sure my lifelong interest in craft and sewing started back there in that lady's tent.

As expected, Wayne and I were enrolled at the local Mitta Mitta Junction Primary School, about a mile up the road from the dam. It was a one room two-teacher school with only about thirty students. No school uniforms or shoes here either! The majority of students were migrants who were bussed daily from the Bonegilla Migrant Camp. Wayne and I walked to and from school along a long, winding, dirt road besides which grew a giant fig tree laden with ripe fruit. Every afternoon we'd feast on these juicy fruits on our way home from school.

We settled in easily, and within no time were making friends with the migrant children. They were friendly and sociable, and the language barrier didn't seem to be a problem. Some of the girls my age were students of dance and since I was continually pestering them, they taught me a few dance steps during recess periods. We'd gather in a group under the trees in the schoolyard and they'd choreograph some simple little lunchtime concerts I could participate in. Since I'd always yearned to learn dancing, being part of these little shows made me feel accepted and part of the group.

The real excitement for me though was the interschool sports carnival in Albury, that the school participated in a few months after we arrived. When I won two trophies, a cup and saucer and plate set for the hundred yards sprint, and three small lamb figurines for the 200 yards event. I felt very proud of myself. The trophies were a far cry from the elaborate trophies youngsters receive today, yet they are precious to me and remain the only treasures I've managed to retain of my early life. While I've been lucky to have collected a few more accolades since then, these two treasures are the most precious.

Another surprise! Another disappointment! By midyear, we were once again moving on. This time, headed for Melbourne, Victoria. Dad and Mum had recently befriended a Melbourne couple, Leo and Kath, who were holidaying at the weir. It took very little to convince Dad to once more pack up the family and head further south. Leo said we could park our caravan in their backyard in Lalor until Dad found employment and a more permanent home for the caravan. Once more, there were sad goodbyes to my new school friends and my lovely lady friend at the camping ground. Two new schools and far too many sad goodbyes already, and it was only mid-year.

Chapter 9

Melbourne – More Sexual Abuse

What a reception awaited us in Melbourne. We were welcomed by a shock of ice-cold winter weather we'd never previously experienced. And coming from Queensland, our summer wardrobe certainly wasn't up to the task of keeping us warm. Leo, our host, suggested we'd be more comfortable staying inside their house in Lalor, warmed by a wood fire roaring away in the lounge room. My parents were of course suitably pleased to sleep inside, instead of the draughty caravan. But, unfortunately, there was no room inside for me! Despondently, I was relegated to sleep alone in the caravan parked in the backyard. I never understood why Mum didn't object. I was eleven years old and I'd always slept in the same bed as Wayne—I'd never been alone at night. Even though I wasn't afraid of the dark, I felt rejected, unhappy and anxious out there by myself.

Was there something that emanated from me, a silent signal, saying I was fair game for predators? Or had this man, Leo, picked up on some predatory vibe from Dad? On my first night alone in the caravan, Leo came knocking. Once he came inside, he began touching me and trying to fondle me. I'd experienced enough from Dad to know what he wanted. I was so terrified of him that I started crying uncontrollably. Mercifully, my crying scared him off, but I was left feeling confused, afraid and unprotected.

It was distressing, not being able to tell anyone about Leo's visit. I naturally assumed Mum's dismissal of Dad's abuse six months earlier proved that no one would believe me, especially not her. Consequently, I was in a constant state of apprehension, wondering what might lie ahead in the nights to come. After that encounter I always locked the caravan door securely when I went to bed; but that didn't prevent Dad's nocturnal visits, he had a key to the door.

Thankfully, within a few months, Dad obtained a caretaker job at a factory in Thomastown nearby, where we could park our caravan. I'd been spending every night constantly on guard, wondering what might happen if Leo came knocking again; worried that next time my tears might not scare him off so easily. Unfortunately for me though the factory site, with its many buildings and alleyways, gave Dad many areas where he would instruct me to meet him to continue his abuse.

We were soon enrolled at the Thomastown Primary School; I was in Grade six, Wayne Grade three. It was yet again a totally different environment, and I was once more made to change my writing style. But the great news was; no uniforms. Initially, everyone's obsession with football surprised me; everyone wanted to know what football team we barracked for, but I hadn't a clue about football. Nevertheless, I was fascinated with everyone's colourful hand-knitted pullovers, socks, scarves, beanies, and gloves, all in their favourite team's colours. The merchandise marketing of today hadn't yet taken hold, so everything was handmade.

The effort of getting to school was a mission. From the factory site, we'd have to traipse across a neighbouring field where we risked life and limb. That's how it felt anyway when we were butted by the neighbours angry Billy goat or swooped on by territorial magpies living in the lone gum tree. Winter saw us trudging through soggy knee-high grass and mud, to get to the footpath beside the roadway. We'd then walk about a mile (1.6 km) beside the roadway to school. Many times, we were chastised for being late for assembly or reprimanded for wearing gumboots – yes, shoes again – instead of school shoes which were, of course, in our bags to change into.

Our time in Melbourne didn't include much socialising, apart from an occasional visit to Leo and his family. I'm sure there were many good times, but I remember few, apart from going to Luna Park once and riding on the big dipper. However, 1956 was an exciting time to be in Melbourne, especially when black and white television first arrived. We'd drive down to the local shops and gather with a group of other excited people outside the store window where a television was set up, to watch the few available programs screening at night. Later on, we had the absolute thrill of sitting in our neighbours lounge room witnessing the Melbourne Olympic broadcast on their new television set. At such times we can be grateful for the smallest pleasures as they can be the sweetest.

How fortunate I was back then to accumulate such wonderful memories. Being able to bear witness to the world's greatest athletes performing on the world's stage. I'll never forget seeing the young Dawn Frazer and Murray Rose make their marks on the world stage of swimming. Later, my early passion to run was intensified as I witnessed our inspiring athletes. To my young self, it was almost too exciting to bear, watching Shirley Strickland and Betty Cuthbert perform so magnificently before me on the screen. It was magical, a dream come true. I felt inspired. This was what I'd always dreamed of: becoming an athlete, a champion. I too just wanted to run.

Many years later, when my own children were members, and I was assistant coach, of the Mackay Athletics Club, our future champion Cathy Freeman was a member. I saw this lovely eleven-year old, as I had once been, starting out on her journey to become a world and Olympic champion. Reflecting on my own journey, I did often wonder what might have been if my eleven-year old self had been given the opportunity to pursue my own dream. Nevertheless, I accepted long ago it wasn't the path I was meant to take. There were other adventures and challenges ahead of me and I have no lingering regrets of what might have been. Perhaps in my next lifetime, I'll get that opportunity if it's meant to be.

Meanwhile, attending Thomastown Primary school was a happy phase of my life, I really felt I was where I belonged, at last. In six short years, I'd experienced twelve schools that I remembered clearly and very many more I'd attended when we were travelling with the carnival (approximately twenty-six in all). Prior to Melbourne, the longest period I'd attended one school was two years. After six months living in Melbourne, I finally felt at home. There were no indications things would not go on as they had for the last six months. Of course, back then, children were 'seen and not heard,' so we weren't privy to our parents' conversations or thoughts on life. So, in my childhood innocence, I lived with a false feeling of security, drifting along in my own happy little world. I had no idea what lay ahead at the end of the school year, although I shouldn't have been surprised.

Chapter 10

The Worst Possible News

It was the worst possible news; the school year was finished, we were leaving Melbourne. This news hit me hard; I couldn't believe it. It wasn't because we were leaving anyone in particular; I'd only cultivated a few friendships at school and I'd never attended birthday parties because I was too self-conscious to go alone. It was more about my lost educational opportunity. I'd finished top of my Grade six class and I'd earned a scholarship to high school or technical college. I was crushed; this was bad news! I tried to look for the positives, even though I couldn't see any at the time. I knew how many schools I'd attended over my short lifetime—three schools just in that year—so I tried to remain as optimistic as any eleven-year-old could. I knew my schooling would continue somewhere else. Never for one moment did it occur to me that this school might be my last.

After this disappointment, it then turned out to be an ideal Christmas holiday period for Wayne and me at the Red Cliffs Caravan Park near Mildura, Victoria. Every day was adventure-filled, with other kids in the park. We'd spend hours at the local swimming pool most days and the Saturday movie matinees were the highlight of the week. When the school year arrived, I was enrolled in Grade seven at the Red Cliffs High School. As usual, I was nervous about starting a new school, but I was excited too. I loved it from the first day; every day seemed like a dream and I couldn't wait to get there. And there was the bonus of learning French.

Then, as abruptly as the dream began, it ended. After only a week, Mum, in her cool unemotional way, informed me I'd be leaving school; we were going grape picking. She then directed me to tell the school principal that afternoon I wouldn't be returning to school. My god, I can still see my small, sad, eleven-year-old self, standing against the wall outside the principal's office, too afraid to knock. After what seemed like an eternity, a kind female staff member saw me—terrified—standing there and asked what was wrong. After I explained that my mother said I had to see the principal to tell him I was leaving school she knocked on the door and escorted me into the principal's office.

As I entered the principal's expansive office and saw him sitting behind his big wooden desk, I was overcome with such fear that I burst into tears. Between sobs, I managed to get my explanation out, as best as an eleven-year old could, only to be told I had to attend school: it was the law. I said, 'We're going grape picking, I won't be able to.' I then felt even more worried.

With the gift of hindsight, and being a mother myself, I find it difficult to fathom Mum's lack of awareness in giving me such responsibility. Having to leave school was disappointing enough. Surely Mum could have shown more empathy and shielded me from the confrontation with the authorities. She seemed totally oblivious of my youth and immaturity and failed to support me in my time of disappointment.

After that, life as it had been, for all of us, changed forever. I turned twelve mid-way through our first grape picking season and life no longer had the quality of childhood. Reality took on a new meaning; I'd now joined the adult world of work. I was afforded no special treatment, and for someone my size, working in the extreme heat and trying to keep up with the adults was grueling. The grape bunches were cut off the vines with small knives, similar to a pocket knife, only razor sharp. I also had to learn to use the sharpening stone to maintain my knife's sharpness. Not many of us avoided the misfortune of having a finger wrapped up after accidently slicing it with the knife.

After picking, the sultana grapes were dipped in an alkaline solution before being spread out on hessian racks to dry in the sun. There was continual pressure to get the crop in because the weather would often change without notice. There was added stress knowing that the extreme heat would cause the grapes to ripen too quickly.

The air from the north, lacking in humidity, would be dry and harsh, oppressive and still, without a whiff of a breeze to cool us during the day or night. Some days when we broke for lunch, the temperature was recorded at 120 degrees Fahrenheit (50 degrees Celsius) in the shade. There was no talk of global warming sixty years ago; these extreme temperatures were normal and were, from memory, rarely reported. Another common occurrence was the red dust storms that blew in from the west, covering everything in their path. More than likely, these extreme weather conditions were rarely reported because bringing attention to such extremes could have discouraged many a prospective grape picker.

Soon after starting our first grape picking season Mum registered me with the Victorian Correspondence School and during that first grape season, I began Grade seven. Being able to continue my education was a relief. However, working five days a week left little time for study so I studied at night or on our days off. Often in between jobs and travel, I managed to catch up on some neglected schoolwork. I was literally on my own; Mum had very little input into my studies, and Dad wasn't literate enough to help me. Not that he would have wanted to anyway.

While I loved the study, I often found it difficult to keep focused and committed to my studies while working the long hours we did. Although it seemed at times I'd never get there, I somehow managed to complete two grades of study in three years. And at the end of Grade eight, my 98% pass seemed a just reward for my perseverance.

By now I was fifteen years old, enthusiastic, and still enjoying the learning. I had great expectations for further study so enrolled to study Grade 9. However, the workload was too overwhelming, with Dad refusing to take on any employment that didn't also involve me. I decided to cease my studies after only a few months. Although I tried to not dwell on it I confess I did feel ripped off. It took a lot of mental self-talk to keep my educational dream alive, by continually telling myself that I'd one day continue my education. I couldn't let go of the dream, the vision of what I believed I was capable of.

Even though my life went on at a steady pace, my feelings of not measuring up obsessed me. Even though work accolades continued over the years, what I wanted and desired still evaded me; to become someone worthwhile through education; to be acknowledged for my intellect; that was what I truly desired. I continually questioned, how could I prove to myself, if not to the world, that I did have what it takes to succeed if I wasn't educated?

When I say 'Have a dream and then hold on to it, keeping it ever in your vision,' I speak from experience. My desire to complete my education consumed my thoughts for many years. Somewhere inside me, I knew if I had the chance I could do it. I knew, in my inner core, if I didn't give up on my dream I would somehow, sometime, and in some way achieve my desire.

It wasn't until I'd had a long and successful career and a family that I was at last able to take the gamble and take the great plunge into study. I am so proud and grateful that I didn't give in to the inevitable self-doubts and naysayers and chose instead to stick to the task before me.

Thankfully, education eventually opened doors to my new life, previously unimagined. That, however, was in my future. Now, my life was one of work, and education was a dream I had to nurture for many long years before I would, at last, have the feeling of fulfilment and personal satisfaction I craved.

Chapter 11

Who's Looking Out For Me?

After only one season of grape picking, the itinerant lifestyle grabbed a hold of Dad once more. And having me—a capable and seemingly willing worker—made it even more attractive, I'm sure. Now, he had someone who could help support his penchant for regular car upgrades, along with his intention of replacing the old homemade caravan with a modern one.

Within a few weeks of the grape season ending, the winter chill arrived, and once again we were on the move looking further afield for work. We relocated to Nangiloc, a small-crop farming area along the Murray River, not far from Mildura. We found work with a local farmer and chose a camping area near to the property. We set up our campsite high above the ochre-red cliffs overlooking the magnificent fast-flowing Murray River below. It was exhilarating, scurrying down the cliff face looking for a safe spot to sit and fish. The Murray, as it was referred to by the locals, was abundant with Murray cod and redfin, and since Dad was a keen fisherman we had many meals of this tasty fare.

The rich fertile soil grew lettuces and cabbages: lush, large, and sweet-tasting. Our job was to harvest the lettuces and cabbages and pack them, ready for market, as well as weeding and thinning out carrot seedlings. The work wasn't difficult; just mundane and repetitive as most seasonal work tended to be. There was an unfortunate downside, too. Each morning before daybreak, the farmer would turn on the overhead sprinklers to wash the frost and ice from the crops before the sun rose.

Unlike the extreme heat of the grape-picking season, we were now working in wet and freezing temperatures. For this work, unlike grape picking, where we were paid based on our productivity, we were earning a wage. Since I was being paid a woman's wage, I was expected to do a woman's work. Before equal pay for equal work was mandated, men earned three pounds ($6.00) a day, women two pounds ten shillings ($5.00).

Some of the work may have had many unpleasant aspects, but our living environment and the healthy outdoor lifestyle was amazing. As the sun rose, and the morning light filtered dazzlingly through the tree branches, many varieties of birds chorused us awake with their cheerful tunes. Living under the canopy of trees on the river bank afforded us excellent protection from any inclement weather and any unwanted strangers wandering in the vicinity. We were never troubled by the odd poor alcoholic who bedded down on the river bank, under the cover of trees at night, after sipping a few methylated spirits and orange cocktails.

This secluded environment was also ideal because it afforded Dad many opportunities to continue his nocturnal abuse under the cover of darkness. By now, the abuse had taken on a more intimidating and threatening tone. The demands were more sinister, now that I was older. 'Be ready to 'give me one' tonight,' was to be his command whenever he wanted sex. Dad abused me so regularly he knew my menstruation cycle. When I said I hadn't finished he'd tell me I'd had them 'so' many days and should be finished by now. He'd often joke, in his cruel way, suggesting I might be pregnant. He used no form of protection, and for a long time, I did fear becoming pregnant.

After finishing the contract in Nangiloc, we relocated back to the Red Cliffs Caravan Park as Dad had decided to go rabbit trapping out west of Mildura. The rabbits were in plague proportions on many of the properties and he'd been told he could make a good living trapping them. This venture entailed camping for several nights in the bush until he'd trapped enough rabbits for the carrier to pick up. I was overjoyed; he'd be gone for days and I'd be safe with Mum and Wayne in the caravan park.

But, another surprise awaited me; he hadn't planned on doing this on his own. He insisted he'd need me to accompany him on these overnight trips! Although I pleaded with Mum to stay with her and Wayne, my pleas fell on deaf ears. With a sinking heart, I knew what his ulterior motive was; and I was certainly proven right.

Why did Mum let me go? I don't know! Here I was: a twelve-year-old, walking around the bush at all hours of the night, with only a lantern for a companion. Every few hours I'd be woken to make my rounds of the traps, remove the rabbits, break their necks, reset the traps and continue the round. There was always that eerie and frightening feeling of walking alone in this strange, dark environment and hearing the night noises of the bush just beyond the lantern light.

The result of my disrupted sleep pattern also meant I grew tired. Each time we returned I'd plead with Mum to let me stay home. My young mind kept questioning why she wouldn't listen to me. Surely, she remembered what I'd told her about Dad's abuse over a year ago. I then realised there was no one looking out for me. I felt alone, afraid, and totally helpless.

Through my research and study over time, I've learned how difficult it can be for many sexual abuse victims to move beyond the torment. A despoiling of one's body can be hard to accept, yet the mental pain can, in fact, be more debilitating than the physical. How does a victim rid oneself of the memories and the mental torment that so often accompanies the physical assault? With no one to count on for support, and not having a coping strategy to counteract the flashbacks, many are driven to self-harm. Something as simple as a smell or a touch can trigger deep-seated, and thought to be forgotten, memories.

Maybe I was one of the lucky ones, as I know there are many others who experienced more horrific abuse than I did. Perhaps I coped better than countless others because I could take myself off through disassociation. I'd take my mind in to another space during the abuse. And perhaps because deep down I believed it wouldn't go on forever. I wanted to hold on to that; I did believe it would end, someday. It's true, you cling to the things that get you through, and my coping strategy was reading books. Providing I could read, I could transport myself away from my reality, and immerse myself in stories of adventure; of boarding school; of other lands and times.

Was this my way of dissociating myself from the reality of my life? Definitely! Reading allowed me to not think about or dwell on the 'now.' Reading kept me from dwelling on the fear of my secret coming out.

Reading was my escape hatch. Reading has been the one constant throughout my life; the one thing that I could take comfort in and rely on.

The abuse became a continuing pattern over the following six years. There was always intimidation, and threats of violence of what he'd do to me if I told anyone. Dad's demands were risky and foolish. He'd demand I meet him behind a tree; behind the car; or some secretive spot on a riverbank; in the bush; and even behind a tree in a caravan park. At other times he'd insist I go for a car ride for some obscure reason – after which he'd pull off the road somewhere and abuse me. As I grew older, he told me he shouldn't have to ask, I should come to him and offer him 'one.' Often when I didn't turn up at the appointed spot, he'd later creep into the annex where Wayne and I slept and shake me awake. Each time my innermost mind would be crying out, *Mum, please help me!* But, Mum never came.

Time and again when Dad was badgering me, I'd declare, 'You won't be doing this to me next year.' And of course, he'd always agree – it was his way of shutting me down! But, I knew in my heart he never for one moment meant it, and I never really believed it would stop soon either. He showed no remorse or guilt on his part for the wrong he was doing, he appeared to have no capacity for either. In fact, he saw the abuse as his right, and he was totally incapable of displaying any emotion that showed he cared about anyone other than himself. Over the years, I tried desperately to protect Wayne from the horror of what was happening. That was the main reason I'd acquiesce, agreeing to meet Dad anywhere away from Wayne's presence in the annex. The years wore on endlessly, but I never lost hope that one day the abuse would stop. I just didn't know how far away that 'one day' was.

It was many years before I was to learn the truth of how much Wayne had witnessed. To learn that he had been, for years an impotent bystander, was devastating. Not until we were in our forties, and discussing our past, did Wayne tell me how for many years he'd been deeply troubled. But like me, he had been powerless to stop it. It also saddened me to admit that I had been a witness to Dad's endless bullying and ridicule. I told Wayne that if I'd realised the extent of his knowledge, we could have run away together, disappeared. Wayne just looked at me and reiterated my own thoughts over the years, 'We couldn't run away. We had nowhere to go and no one to go to.'

Chapter 12

Our Travel Traumas

A s the years rolled one into another, we traipsed back and forth between states, chasing the seasons. Although travelling gave us a break from the work, for Wayne and me the long days of travel were tedious and boring. I wonder if Mum and Dad dreaded it as much as we did. With the gift of hindsight, I'm sure the reason the travel days were dreaded was that we were embarrassed by Dad's churlish displays. With a cigarette hanging from the corner of his mouth he'd yell and tell us to, 'Get rid of all this shit we're carrying around the country.' What made it worse was that other pickers, who already regarded him poorly and simply avoided him, would witness his foolish rantings.

Getting ready for the trip was a nightmare. There was always, of course, some preliminary packing done the day before departure, but the real work happened the morning we headed off. Everything that could be was securely locked away in cupboards. The final task was placing the big wash tub—used for bathing and washing—in the middle of the caravan floor and then piling it high with everything that didn't fit in cupboards. Considering our lifestyle, this was a major undertaking as everything we owned was packed into the caravan or car.

Dad just never got the hang of packing up for travel. All would start off well, then chaos would reign as he'd haphazardly toss things into the two vehicles. Then out of nowhere, when things didn't fit, his arrogance and impatience would surface; he'd snap and have a nasty temper tantrum which was as frightening and as black as his outward demeanour. He'd slam things around and scream verbal abuse and then kick the vehicle as if it was at fault. Finally, Mum would take control and bring a little sanity to the situation, while he took off and left us to finish it.

Dad's brain snaps weren't the only spectacle. On many occasions, we were undoubtedly the sight of the day when Mum, Wayne and I would follow up behind the caravan with large stones ready to chock behind the wheels each time the old Buick jumped out of gear and stalled on the hill. Apart from it being dangerous, it was doubly embarrassing with Dad yelling abuses out the window of the car. Eventually, he purchased a Chrysler Wayfarer utility, which eliminated that problem. It also meant that the extra bits and pieces that cluttered the caravan could be packed in the tray of the utility.

While the Chrysler looked nice and was proudly exhibited for all to see, we were faced with a total seating reorganisation. Us kids no longer had the comfort of the back seat to lounge on during travel. Now the four of us were squashed into the front of the utility. In the days of the bench seat spread across the width of the cabin, it was virtually impossible to feel comfortable. Wayne and I continued to grow into young adults as the cabin seemed to grow increasingly smaller.

I was the one who Dad insisted sit next to him, wedged under his armpit. Beside me sat Wayne, then Mum on the far side with the dog at her feet and the cat perched up behind our heads on the console. Four people plus animals squeezed into a vehicle which was, unlike our modern and comfortable air-conditioned vehicles, nightmarish. This arrangement became a never-ending battle of patience and will. My occasional request to change seating fell on deaf ears and in the end, I gave up asking.

The travel days were mind-numbing, with only the countryside for entertainment. Dried grass as far and the eye could see covered the fields. Just a few metres from the roadside, cattle or sheep grazed in ignorance of our boredom. It was a never-ending, never-changing highway, which, in the extreme heat of summer, the mirages shimmering up ahead tricked us into believing we were headed into an ocean. These trips, more often than not, took many wearisome days of travel before we arrived at our often interstate destination. On these longer trips, we'd pull off the highway before sunset to set up camp for the night. Tired and drained mentally, physically, and emotionally, we'd have to unload our multitude of belongings in the centre of the caravan, before Mum could prepare our evening meal. Then with only a cursory wash of face and hands we'd fall into our beds exhausted.

For me, traveling held no fascination at all; all I wanted to do was just sit and read. But this was impossible with the four of us crammed into the front seat. Mum was continually harping on about my head always being stuck in a book; she thought I should be enjoying the scenery as we drove. But, to me, it was just an endless, monotonous highway surrounded on all sides by a landscape of trees and grass as far as the eye could see. Our work environment was similar with hundreds of acres of crops of one kind or another. Unlike Mum, I had no interest whatsoever in nature while travelling; I saw enough of it while working. And anyway, reading was my escape into another world. It kept me from thinking about the nights.

Summer travel was dreadful. With the car windows down, we'd be assailed by a continual stream of hot air blasting around the cabin which failed to cool either tempers or bodies. And, because I was squashed under Dad's armpit, I felt hotter than everyone else. At least I thought I was. When the extreme humidity within the cabin got to everyone, Dad would reluctantly allow Wayne or me to travel in the back. It was always such a relief to lie on a mattress in the back of the Ute under the Tonneau cover out of the wind; I could read to my heart's content. I had to be extra careful though because if I sat up to enjoy some fresh air and Dad thought I was attracting too much attention from the truck drivers following behind us it, I'd be hauled back in front.

Winter travel, on the other hand, could be more enjoyable. I confess to being quite impressed and a tad more interested in the surroundings. With frost or snow covering the countryside as far as the eye could see, it was a glorious sight to behold. On an early morning drive, with the air crisp and clear, and with sheep and cattle grazing silently in the ice-covered fields, the countryside had a picture-book appearance. The remoteness and beauty of the landscape gave off the impression of an untouched and untroubled land. This cold silent landscape did capture my interest and I always marvelled at the way the warm early-morning sun streaming down upon the moist earth could create a misted halo effect as it rose from the ground. Now this, a truly beautiful sight, was something I did appreciate!

Yet, there were drawbacks to the winter travel which often overrode the highlights. Sure, the outside landscape was picture perfect, but inside the vehicle was a different matter altogether. Four bodies and two animals crammed inside the cabin with the windows wound up and the heater on was not something that evokes good memories. The stuffiness this created would be overpowering, and the humidity within caused condensation to build up on the windows. After the windscreen fogged up it would be necessary to use the de-mister, which further exacerbated the problem.

There was never any conversation between us and with no radio or travel games we had nothing to occupy us while we travelled. I'd often wonder how Mum could enjoy these trips as she appeared to; perhaps it gave her the opportunity to sit and relax, to look into space and perhaps daydream of better times.

Although I was young and not aware of the world of adults, I developed a sense of empathy for Mum. I often wondered how it must feel for a mother to have to prepare a meal and a bed at the end of the day of travel. I would love to have talked to her about it, to learn how she felt, and what her philosophies on life were, or if she, in fact, had any. She never let me into her inner world and so the years moved on and I never got to know her inner thoughts.

I knew for sure I didn't want to get married and have that kind of life thrust upon me. It was only some years later, when I became a mother myself, that I could look back on those days with true understanding. Through experience, I learned that mothers just got on with it, that's what mothers had to do. I soon learned too, like Mum no doubt did, that there was no use in complaining, it was just best to get on with what was required and do it.

Chapter 13

He Was Bad To The Core

I've told a lot about him, but not enough to show who Dad really was, deep down in his soul. I'd often wondered over the years; *What motivated him? What did he really feel and think?* To us he was a soulless person who showed no empathy or compassion to person or animal. In fact, he appeared to enjoy seeing the pain and anguish that others suffered. There was no sense of remorse or apology either. He took great joy in ridiculing mum and us kids, sniggering and laughing as he witnessed our misery. Over time he succeeded in greatly eroding our self-esteems. Wayne and I recall no good memories of him, in fact our memories of him consist mainly of contempt and fear. Letting go of those feelings have been some of the biggest challenges we've both had to face.

Wayne and I were always mindful of his moods and fearful of his abruptly-triggered anger. When angry, his lips would stretch into a wide line and his cruel words would be hurled forth. To both of us, he was physically, emotionally, and verbally abusive. Anything could tip him off, and when angered, he would just lash out. It's been said that people who are kind to animals are kind to people; those who treat animals poorly also treat people poorly. This was so true in our situation; he was a sad excuse for a man and a father.

We had a little Corgi Fox Terrier cross called Skippy; a happy little fellow who we adored. An unfortunate habit he had was to sneak out from under the caravan steps and nip a person's heels as they exited. They'd get a bit of a fright, but he wasn't vicious and never broke the skin. He just let people know they were intruders. Dad's immediate reaction was always the same—he'd lash out with his boot and kick Skippy hard. There was also the odd occasion when Skippy would take off for the night, looking for girlfriends. On his return the next morning, Dad, who never took into account it was a dog's nature to do this, would just give Skippy a good thrashing. During one of our overland trips, when we'd stopped for lunch, Skippy took off over a nearby hill and didn't look back. Although we waited and called for hours, the little fellow had no doubt suffered enough abuse, and obviously decided to take his chances over the other side of the hill.

Wayne and I got the same treatment; if he couldn't reach out and beat us with his hand, he would strike out with his foot and land a good hard kick wherever he could. Too often, he'd take out his frustration and anger at my lack of acquiescence, on Wayne. Even as a small boy of nine or ten, Wayne was expected to be working diligently in the field, instead of going to school. If, by chance, he happened to be slacking off and daydreaming, as kids do, Dad would slink up behind him and give him a hard kick and tell him to get to work. It was a brutality that was hard to comprehend. It frustrated me too that I was powerless to stop it: I was just a kid myself. Reflecting on that time, perhaps we might have been better off if we could have done what Skippy did; take off over the hill and not look back.

Dad's constant surveillance unnerved me greatly too; no matter where I was, I'd feel his eyes on me. Even in the field, if I happened to work my way too far ahead, he'd call me back. Friendships were discouraged because everyone was a 'rat' in his eyes. If a young man showed me some attention he'd soon be sent packing. Dad also took great joy in ridiculing and making crude personal remarks about me in front of any young man who tried to converse with me. This, of course, caused extreme embarrassment for both of us.

It eventually dawned on me how malevolent he was, keeping me isolated during my crucial teen years. I had many lovely young admirers; respectful and hardworking young men—but they were out of my reach. It mattered not to Dad that I only wanted friendship, they were discouraged from even conversing with me in a general manner and I knew the reasoning behind it. What was more hurtful for me was that Wayne had the freedom to enjoy the unlimited company of his young friends.

Although I don't remember ever crying about it, there were times when I felt terribly sad and helpless. I was often overcome by feelings of loneliness as waves of grey despondency swelled up from deep within, leaving me feeling imprisoned, like Rapunzel trapped in the tower. All I wanted was to be a part of the young group I worked alongside, to bond and get pleasure from similar experiences and interests, but he denied me this all my young working life.

I know he was a flawed being. But I also know little of what came before me; what kind of life or upbringing he had. Perhaps he did love me, in his sick abusive way. Life experience, maturity, and my years studying psychology and human development have given me a deeper understanding of human nature and I've worked hard at forgiving the past. Over time I've sought counselling and therapy from a psychologist, and later a psychiatrist, to break down the barriers I erected to protect my secret, and who I thought I was. The burden of carrying my past hurts around was too heavy to maintain; it made my soul weary.

I've exposed a lot of his immoral traits, yet I, like most children, wanted my father's love. Not the cold-hearted, abusive love he demonstrated, but an innocent love where I felt worthwhile, like a child should. I subconsciously hoped, as I did with Mum, that by working compliantly over the many years I'd gain that authentic love.

Chapter 14

Just Who Were The Pickers?

Just who were the 'pickers' you might ask? I guess, in many ways, we were just modern-day gypsies. As with any population, the pickers consisted of many types of people. Within this unconventional itinerant community, there was a certain level of disparity of types. The larger family groups who saw seasonal work as their life vocation were more sociable and content with their lifestyle. They held no grand design to be other than what or who they were. Often, they included many generations who followed the same nomadic path. As their children grew up and became independent, they too followed the cycle of seasonal work.

There were also many single men—solitary types—who disclosed very little information about themselves. One man in particular comes to mind. Charlie Kahn was an Indian man of indeterminate age, stooped over, or rather folded over, at almost 90 degrees. One could tell he had been a very tall man, but we were never privy to the reason for his disability. He was friendly, but private and very little was known of his former, or for that matter, present life. All we knew was that he turned up each summer in Bathurst and Oberon and was a top pea picker. He cooked on an open fire, as did many of the campers, outside his one-man tent. He was a curiosity to us young folk, who loved to sit and watch him make his Johnny cakes; a thin bread loaf made from a damper-like dough and cooked over coals, which he'd often share with us. I found him fascinating and he was always nice to the young ones.

Then there were the few families who kept isolated from the majority. They were the ones who were seemingly considered to be just a touch above the average. Everything, from their personal attire: sun hats, long sleeve shirts, and work gloves; to their modern and upmarket caravans and vehicles, were well presented; some might even say sterile. I think we fitted somewhere in between.

The interaction most men had with each other was mainly in the field, or over an occasional few beers in the pub when they went to town—women weren't allowed in pubs back then. Often, after arriving for the new season, the pickers would set up temporary camp in the town caravan park while the adults scoured the district for jobs. At night, the youngsters would congregate in the caravan park laundry where we'd listen to the latest music on a small portable record player; so much of it was great happy music. When Dad thought I was having too good a time and there were boys involved, especially after dark, I'd be hauled off home, no questions asked.

I've often wondered what became of all the youngsters I knew back then. It was so many years ago, but it feels like yesterday. Blond haired Fanny; energetic and vibrant. Wendy, who had bad acne and tried desperately to disguise it with all forms of lotions and potions. I remember feeling sorry for her and grateful I wasn't inflicted with acne as she was. And where are Billy, Chum, and Errol, the boys who at some stage during my teen years I had a crush on? I remember their young faces so well and I wonder if life has been kind to them. Have they been fortunate in being able to achieve success and satisfaction in their life choices as I have? I hope so!

Yes, seasonal work was hard; the working week long and tiring. Our work area ranged over many regions from Queensland to South Australia. The summer season usually saw us working for some of the bigger pea growing farmers in the Bathurst, Oberon, and Orange areas of New South Wales, where at the height of the season, there could be as many as one hundred pickers working together in the field. This meant there could be thirty or so youngsters of all ages running around or working in the paddocks.

The pea crops were planted across many hundreds of acres on all types of terrain. We pickers would be spread out across a field of peas, dotted like busy ants spread across an anthill. During the height of summer, it was imperative that the pickers were on hand when the crops were ready. If the crop was left too long on the bush the peas over ripened and dried out, thus were unsalable.

Often there would be as many as three pickings on each field. We'd work through the crops on the first picking, then perhaps a week later, after having done the first pick on another field, we'd return for the second picking. Crops were always staggered to be ready without too much delay between crops. This was the way it worked best and for the bigger farmers who grew hundreds of acres of peas, this often entailed many months of work.

In the Oberon area, an hour's drive from Bathurst, we would often be so high up in the mountains we'd be enveloped by clouds. The clouds were a light fine veil of moisture, dubbed 'mountain mist', that continually floated and swirled down around us, hanging low and cold for days and often weeks at a time. Even though it was summer, and although the sun would try in vain to break through the heavy cloud cover, it was a futile effort. While we worked, great expanses of land were continually being cleared around us—over the mountains, and further down in the valleys—to open up more land for planting. The tree logs and stumps would then be piled into massive stacks and set on fire, often burning for weeks on end.

While we worked in these high mountain areas, we wore wet weather gear which helped ward off the wet, freezing air. During our lunch break, we'd gratefully sit close to the fires where we could warm our freezing bodies. Unfortunately, the wet weather gear, which certainly kept us dry, didn't afford us much basic warmth. Our hands, exposed to the elements, would remain frozen throughout most of the day. Since we couldn't do anything about it, we just accepted that it was a part of the work. There is nothing like frozen fingers to make you appreciate holding a mug of delicious hot soup; on the coldest days, Mum's thermos flask of homemade soup was a lifesaver.

These mountainous areas often had no road access for our caravans and vehicles, which meant we'd have to camp in a tent on the edge of the forest, making do with lanterns, and cooking and heating water on the open fires. Water was accessed from the abundant springs bubbling up through the ground throughout the forest area. After we'd set up our campsite, Dad would dig a hole over a spring, which then filled up with beautiful, pure, crystal-clear water. Our personal items were kept in cartons and boxes inside the tent, the foodstuffs safely locked away from the cheeky possums. Water for washing and bathing was heated up in a four-gallon drum hung over the open fire. We usually bathed once a week before going to town; in the same big round metal wash tub we used for the weekly washing. At night I had a daily wash in our metal basin.

The valley acreages, like the mountainous areas, were also cleared and heavily cultivated for seasonal crops. Gaining access to these areas was as difficult as getting to the higher areas. Winding its way cautiously down through the forest, on the rocky, rough and treacherous tracks, a blitz truck—an ex-army vehicle— was utilised to transport people down into the valley below.

This was a journey so scary many of us chose to walk rather than ride. Our vehicles were left parked on top of the mountain, while some of the sturdier caravans could be maneuvered down using a tractor or the blitz. As a rule, our campsite in the valley was set up on the flattest area, surrounded on three sides by fields of peas planted on the most uneven, and one would think inaccessible, hillsides.

Seasonal work was very competitive as much of it was piecemeal work; we were paid for the pounds/kilos we harvested. This was the reason we'd be up at daylight and ready to head out to the fields to begin work as the sun poked its golden head over the horizon. Whether the sun greeted us brightly or not—rain, hail, or shine—the crops had to be harvested; we weathered all seasons and took it in our stride. A property owner was always on hand to weigh the bags we'd amassed at the end of each row, then record it in his tally book.

The early morning hustle and bustle of activity was energetic. The pickers, whose caravans and tents were scattered around the camping area, would be moving around their campsites from first light, preparing for the day ahead. If we happened to be lucky, when not up high in the mountains, we could set up camp beside a spring stream for easy access to water, or near a gully within a small group of willow trees. Ordinarily, though, we had to cart our water up in four-gallon drums, from the half-metre wide spring streams which flowed down the hillside. Mum, like the other women, would do the necessary campsite work in the morning before going to the field. The women, as a rule, usually finished earlier to go 'home'—back to the campsite—to prepare the evening meal.

Pea picking was back breaking work. We'd be standing bent over, or moving along on our knees through the rows of peas all day filling four-gallon drums to the top, then walking to the end of the row and pouring it into a hessian bag. We did this over and over; day in, day out; week in, week out. There were times when I felt so tired at days end, I just wanted to go to bed and never get up. Wayne's and my bed in the annex were camp stretchers made up with bedding, which was then covered and wrapped in canvas sheeting to keep out the dust and the cold night air. Unfortunately, it was hellishly hot atmosphere for sleeping during the summer months. Then in winter I remember crawling out of the cocoon of warmth each morning and thinking, *I can't wait to crawl back in tonight.* Luckily, the resilience of youth meant that as morning dawned I'd be ready to begin all over again.

As the intense heat of summer turned to the bitter chill of winter, and then to summer again, we traversed back and forth across the states following the seasonal work. Mostly, we chased the pea crops, but during the in-between seasons we'd source other types of work. The early or late spring would see us picking fruit; cherries in Young, New South Wales, apricots in Shepperton, Victoria, then picking grapes in February, in Mildura, Victoria.

Winter was carrot and lettuce season. Before the advent of mechanical methods of thinning out seedlings in small crops, seasonal workers were employed to do it. Down on hands and knees in the cold, wet soil, fingers plucking out carrot and lettuce seedlings every few inches, we'd work for eight hours each day. Winter also brought other vegetable crops, and for a couple of seasons we worked in the Lockyer Valley, west of Brisbane, harvesting onions and potatoes.

Onions were always loosened in the ground with a machine before we'd walk along the rows, trimming the top and bottom with handheld shears and bagging them, ready for market. Potatoes went through a similar process. Loosened by a tractor, after which we'd fill the four-gallon drums, then carry them to the end of the rows to transfer into hessian bags. This was unpleasantly heavy, dirty, arduous work. Certainly no work for the faint hearted.

Mostly the work entailed continual and repetitive actions, which, when mastered, became natural and automatic. The sooner one learned the basics, the more skilled one became, therefore many were classed as 'gun pickers.' Although I was never a 'gun' in the real sense, I was competent and as good as most adults. It is difficult for me to define what the most difficult task was, as each had an aspect that was hard on a growing body. Climbing a ladder with a canvas bag full of oranges across one's shoulders was very painful; carrying a wide four-gallon drum, cut sideways and filled to the top with cherries, was equally straining on my spine.

No matter the weather or the season, my life of sexual abuse continued. It was a matter of trying to keep focused on my dream of one day being free of this horror. A lesson I learned early on was this; if I didn't like something, and if I couldn't change it, I'd just put my head in neutral and get on with it. Neale Donald Walsch hadn't yet written his three-book series, *Conversations with God*, but after reading it in the 1990's, I agreed with his suggestion that 'What's happening is merely what's happening. How we feel about it is another matter.' An attitude I believe I already had, and one that often came in handy later in my life.

Chapter 15

Fridays – Town Day

Friday. Come on Friday! After the week labouring from sunrise until sundown, our one day off was embraced whole-heartedly. It was an opportunity for the adults to relax and the young ones to be kids. A day when we teenagers didn't have to count how many bags of peas we'd picked that day; or how many rows we'd dragged our buckets along. Friday was the day workers threw off the denims and t-shirts, donned their finest outfits, and headed to town. The older boys with cars always got away early, no doubt to enjoy doing boy things away from their parents' scrutiny.

We might have been isolated, but most of my teenage friends were aware of the latest hair styles and clothes fashions worn by the city youth. The girls would deck themselves out in circular skirts over many layers of colourful tulle or rope petticoats. Gone were the bare feet or sandshoes worn in the fields, out came their wedges; the girls' favourite footwear. To complete the transformation, long hair, tied up under hats throughout the working week, was washed, brushed, and carefully backcombed into the latest fashionable beehives.

Not to be outdone, the boys were as fashion conscious as the girls. En masse, dressed in their black jeans and bright shirts, they'd set out for town. Some of the older boys wore their jeans so tight they literally had to sew the legs up after pouring themselves in. Of course, when it came to hairdo's, the boys were just as determined to present an image equally as impressive as the girls. Their hair, in the Elvis Presley, Brylcreemed hairstyle, most popular in the 1950's and 1960's, was combed and re-combed as they checked their reflections in the shop windows as they strutted through town. Fridays meant they could be regular teenagers; they could throw off the picker label for just a short time, at least in their own eyes. Being itinerant and uneducated certainly didn't deter the youngsters when it came time for having fun.

While in town, they'd also let their hair down for hours at the rock and roll dances. Unfortunately, and frustratingly, these dances were a no-go zone for me. Each week, like clockwork, the girls would ask Mum if I could come with them, but each week Mum's answer was always the same, 'Ask your father.' She knew what his answer would be, and I guess she'd realised by now he made the rules, so she didn't intervene on my behalf.

I loved the modern fashions too, but I wasn't allowed to dress like the other girls. I continually fantasised about brighter and more colourful outfits, but Mum never encouraged me to wear modern clothes – I was obliged to wear the one and only basic uninteresting dress each week when we went to town. When the bodice became too tight on my original dress Mum cut the top off and made a skirt. Because I was embarrassed by looking so girlish and wearing bobby socks, I'd sometimes avoid my young friends when in town. My second dress, when I was sixteen, was a pink affair more suited to a mature older woman and certainly not what could be called fashionable by the youth of the day. By the time I was seventeen I refused to wear the socks, but I still felt as unfashionable as I always had.

But that didn't stop my desire to be like the others. So, it happened, that on one fateful day, my girlfriends finally convinced me I'd look great with a full net petticoat under my skirt. So, after nervously purchasing a three layered, multi- coloured, net petticoat with my few shillings I excitedly joined the girls at the local milk bar. Although I felt a little bashful, I felt like a new person after receiving many complements from the others! Then, from out of nowhere, Dad walked in. When he saw what I was wearing, he let forth a tirade of insults, telling me how ridiculously stupid I looked. I slunk away deeply mortified and ashamed to have my friends witness Dad's embarrassing tirade. Of course, I was instructed to take it off immediately and even though I kept that lovely petticoat for many years, I never wore it again.

As my mid-teens dawned, I continually pleaded for permission to shave my legs, but that request too fell on deaf ears. Dad, as usual, added his penny worth and forbade it, saying no one could notice the hairs. I can laugh about it now, but when I was fifteen my naive attempt to remove the hairs secretly – my goodness, how secret could it be, backfired spectacularly. One day while in town with a few of the girls, I decided to buy some silky mitts to do the job in the caravan park toilets at the edge of town. However, we seriously miscalculated the number of mitts needed or the time it would take to complete the job. So, here I was, in the caravan park toilet, with no mitts left after an hour of rubbing and only one leg completed. Panic set in as the afternoon wore on and I knew very soon I'd be missed.

My wonderful brother, Wayne, then twelve years old, came to my rescue by agreeing to go to the pharmacy for more. My god, what a comedy of errors! When I finally finished, my dark, tanned, hairy legs were rendered hairless and deathly white; the mitts having completely removed my suntan along with the hair. How I thought I'd get away with it I don't know. When Dad saw it he absolutely went ape, ridiculing me as usual and forbidding me from doing it again. When I finally plucked up the courage to attempt it again, I was almost nineteen, and like the first attempt it was a disaster. For some reason, I thought I could be creative and skim over the top with a razor to thin them out, and only succeeded in making my legs look like a patchwork quilt. And of course, I had to finish the job.

As a young teen growing into adulthood, it was frustrating that Mum didn't seem to be in touch with my teenage needs. Even though I worked like an adult, she seemed oblivious to my emerging maturity, and my wish to be like other girls my age. I was naive and fearful of confrontation and anger. I couldn't and didn't argue because, if thwarted, Mum's words could be crueler than Dad's. Besides, arguing was useless, there'd be no discussion or compromise. I've thought, in hindsight, perhaps I've overdramatised it; maybe it's my memory playing tricks on me. But Wayne agrees: both our parents were at fault. Unfortunately, we knew Dad's reasons, but we didn't know Mum's. I think she just took the easy way out.

Chapter 16

What Isolation Really Feels Like

To an observer, I was a normal young girl; I displayed no negative behaviours and was generally outgoing and friendly. I gave no outward perception of how the abuse was affecting me. Yet, I was disturbed and particularly distressed by Dad's constant surveillance; it unnerved me as much as the sexual abuse. This was something that affected how I approached any future relationships. Eventually, it got to the point where if I was with my friends in town I'd duck out of sight when I saw him coming, Often, I'd be caught off guard; he'd appear out of nowhere and announce, 'Mum's looking for help with the shopping.' Later, when I finally caught up with her, she'd say she didn't need me at all. This was just another of Dad's strategies to isolate me from other young people.

Regularly, my friends would ask me to go dancing with them, but Dad's answer was always, 'No, we're going home.' Later, he'd take me aside to tell me there was no point even thinking of going dancing: unless I 'gave him one' we'd definitely be going home. With those words, the familiar feeling of disappointment would flood in. As usual, I'd ask the same well-worn question. 'Why? Mum and Wayne are expecting to go to the pictures?' His answer? 'Give me one, and we'll stay for the pictures.' A well of rage and wretchedness would twist my gut and overwhelm me each time this scenario unfolded. The reality of it was – it made no difference if I agreed or not, he'd get it anyway, he always did. It was his way of bringing me back to reality, reminding me he was in control.

The Friday night pictures were a big event in our lives; a night out which didn't end until 11.30pm or midnight. It was a full program starting with a news reel of current world events; a cartoon; trailers of upcoming movies; then the first movie, followed by a twenty-minute interval. Finally, the second and main movie of the night. Sadly, I'd be seated between Mum and Dad up the back of the theatre while Wayne sat with his friends down the front. I was also forbidden to go out of the theatre during interval. The one occasion I did, Dad followed me out, and catching me talking to a boy angrily pulled me away promising me it wouldn't be happening again. And it didn't.

I never fully enjoyed the second movie knowing we'd be going home soon. I'd sit there in my seat too full of anxiety and dread, thinking about the price I'd be paying for this entertainment. I'd feel an overpowering sense of desperation and shame knowing what was to come. I'd feel like screaming out loud and never stopping; running as fast and as far as I could to get away. The piper would have to be paid: it would probably be tomorrow night. But I knew running away wouldn't help me, there was simply nowhere to go and no one to go to.

Dad wasn't the only sexual predator I had to contend with during my mid-teens. There was Dad's friend Jimmy G. who would sidle up beside me while I was working on a row of peas ahead of Dad. He'd talk about how he had taught his two nephews to have sex with their sister and how he'd like me to join them. On a number of occasions, he dropped his penis out in front of me in an effort to persuade me.

Why was I singled out? I'm sure it was because I was isolated from the other young ones who usually worked together in a group, laughing and talking all day. Why didn't I get away from him? There was no way I could – I'd be working a row of peas dragging a drum along within sight of Dad, so it was impossible to just take off. I realise now that he was a paedophile who was attracted to my physical immaturity. I of course told no one, thus I was left with a deep fear of middle-aged males and it was only after I reached middle age, that the fear and distrust of older men subsided.

How strange is human nature; our innate struggle for self-preservation. As the years rolled by, I continued to hope and pray my silent pleas for escape would be heard by someone, somewhere. As each year came and went, I continued to wonder when this abuse would cease. How many times had I managed to pluck up the boldness and the courage to tell Dad, 'You won't be doing this to me next year.' And each time he'd give the same glib answer, 'No, I won't.' Adding to the lie that was my life. How often had I screamed within my mind, *Mum please help me. Mum please love me. Mum please listen to me.* Deep within me I sought answers – why can't Mum hear my pleas for comfort. But the answers never came.

Chapter 17

Then – Another Secret Unfolds

Control can take many guises and unfortunately for me, Dad's habit of showing a more favourable attitude toward me, especially in front of Mum and Wayne, caused a lot of friction. They believed I was his pet: his favourite. But behind the scene he was a different animal. I was accustomed to his aggressive attitude when we were alone, but his violent outburst one particular day came as a complete shock. We were walking up a hill in the cool hush of evening, slowly making our way home after a long day in the field. I was reveling in and watching the last of the sunlight slip behind the horizon, feeling thankful the long day had ended.

And as usual, I was engrossed in thoughts of the current book I was reading, when out of the blue came the command, 'Be ready to give me one tonight.' This demand always filled me with dread. I knew, ultimately, I had no choice—my years of experience had shown who was in charge. But that didn't stop me. As usual, my automatic response was, 'No,' and as usual the threats and intimidation followed. But, this time he was angrier and more calculating. This time, he disclosed something that was—until then—a secret he and Mum meant to keep.

'Thank Christ you're not mine,' he screamed, his small dark eyes bulging and his thin lips a streak across his deeply suntanned face. His outburst shocked me. Momentarily my mind went blank, then I felt the bewilderment. *What was he saying? Is this another one of his horrible insults to hurt me?*

'What do you mean?'

'Just what I said, thank Christ you're not mine.'

'What do you mean, I'm not yours?'

'I mean, you're not mine, you're adopted.' This time with venom in his voice.

Confusion overtook me, I was literally dumbfounded. I wasn't worldly, I knew very little about anything, especially adoption. I knew only what I'd been told: that bad girls who got in to 'trouble' had to adopt their babies out. What that meant for me I didn't really have time to contemplate; that would come later. *God, how was I supposed to respond to this news? Why hadn't Mum told me?*

It was then the unfolding story took an even crueler twist when he said, 'We adopted you when you were eighteen months old.' He went on to tell me they'd arrived at the orphanage and were given a choice of two little girls; a little redheaded girl, or me who has dark hair. He said Mum wanted the redheaded girl, but he wanted me, and I actually believed him! That was what adopted children were told back then: prospective parents went to the hospital and saw you and picked you out from the others.

'That's why Mum doesn't love you. She wanted the other girl. I'm the only one who loves you.'

It was an overwhelming revelation; but there was more. He went on to tell me, 'When we got you, you had a 'thing' sticking out of your stomach like a man's dick.' Mum had told me the scar circulating my navel had been the result of an umbilical hernia surgery. All the years Dad had been taunting me with 'knowing something' he couldn't tell me I'd worried and wondered if it had been this, and, did it mean I couldn't have babies?

Dad's words naturally had the desired effect, of creating more uncertainty in my mind. *What were Mum's real feelings toward me?* Growing up, I often felt hurt that Mum never cuddled me like she did Wayne; she never showed any real warmth or affection or words of endearment toward me while she obviously adored Wayne. In a way Dad's story made complete sense.

My thoughts travelled back to that long-ago day when I was ten years old. When she said she'd shown the doctor my underpants, and he'd told her someone had been 'interfering' with me, doing something sexual. I'd cried when she had questioned me about doing things with men in the bushes on my way home from school. Although I was fearful of what he might do to me, I said, 'No Mummy, it was Daddy.' Maybe she thought it was my fault! Maybe this was the reason she didn't love me. But I'd only told her because I was frightened of what might happen to me.

Mum had confronted Dad later that night, but he of course denied it; he blamed my eleven-year old cousin Trent. Did she actually believe him? It seemed so; it was as though I was a bystander. She withdrew from me that night, and I was left feeling confused and ashamed. As I lay in bed beside Wayne, feeling unwell, betrayed, abandoned, unloved, and afraid of what Dad's reaction might be, something died in me. Trust is a peculiar thing; It's like a door that stands open—the room grows smaller each time the trust is broken—until one day the door completely closes, and there is trust no more. The belief and trust I had in Mum unconsciously began to die that night, and it was something that I was never able to restore.

In hindsight, it seems that much of my life was defined by stages. My father's cruel outburst that day set the scene for many years of confused and erroneous thoughts. I was awash with a mixture of feelings too; gratified that he wasn't my father, that his blood didn't run through my veins; anger at being rejected by my birth mother at eighteen months; fear, I'd been given to this man, what would become of me?; and sadness, was I so unlovable that I was given away to a new mother who didn't really love me?

Once he had unleashed his tirade and disclosed details of my adoption, he then needed to create a realistic scenario of the circumstances. Whether his story was calculated prior to this outburst I'll never know, but when some years later I was able to discuss my adoption with my Aunt Doreen, Mum's sister, she said it was she who had accompanied Mum to pick me up from the orphanage. Mum had gone down expecting to adopt a newborn baby and instead was offered me.

Looking back, I often wondered if I should have told Wayne about our adoption, but I didn't know how to. He was more than three years younger than me at the time and I wasn't sure how he'd react. And anyway, I was still processing this myself. I wish I had told him when he grew older as he was to find out in an equally cruel way. He was nineteen when he went to the Department of Birth, Deaths, and Marriages to collect his birth certificate before applying for his passport. As she handed the certificate to Wayne, the departmental officer simply stated, 'Of course you're aware you're adopted.' Like me, he was taken aback, but also like me, there was that overwhelming feeling of relief knowing he wasn't tainted with Dad's immorality.

It was a long time before I comprehended how my young mind had been so cruelly manipulated during those formative years. The result of Dad's manipulation was fear and doubt which eroded my self-esteem and sense of self-worth. To eventually understand who I truly was would require genuine self-exploration, self-discovery, and self-revelation. I did a great deal of soul searching and poured over a lot of self-help literature in an effort to understand who I really was, and who I could become. I knew that one day I would need to search for the story of my origins, who I was and where I came from, to gain that understanding. But I wasn't there yet, many years would pass before I could look for the answers I needed.

Chapter 18

Who Was Really Wearing
The Rose Tinted Glasses?

The years just seemed to pass by and before I knew it, it was 1962 and I'd turned seventeen. I knew I needed to make a stand; I had no monetary reward, nothing to show for all my years of toil. I desperately needed an escape from the emotional, sexual, and psychological abuse. I'd had a secret hankering to join the Navy or Air Force, thinking I might be able to perhaps forge a career and make something worthwhile of myself. And I wanted my freedom. So, unknown to Mum and Dad, I sent away for the enlistment paperwork. Naively, I didn't anticipate such a negative reaction when I presented the documents—they wouldn't even consider it. The reason no doubt twofold; he'd lose control of me, and I was a money-making asset.

Not long after that Dad took a trip to Nambour in Queensland to look at a small crop farm he'd seen advertised. I often wondered if this was because he thought it would prevent me from taking off and joining the defense force without his consent. At any rate, he returned filled with elation; he'd purchased the farm – we'd be leaving for the north within a few weeks. For me, the prospect of finally having a real home was intoxicating. No more travelling. No more living in caravans and sleeping in camp stretchers in the annex. It seemed to me an exciting life lay ahead of us. With a grateful heart, I thought, *There'll be no more working in the field. Now, at last, I'll become a normal teenager.*

It just so happened at around that same time Dad, for what reason I don't know, bought a little black Singer Tourer convertible car. It was a temperamental little vehicle and I'd been trying vainly to learn to drive it. Dad wasn't the most patient or skilled driving instructor so I took a number of driving lessons with a professional instructor in Orange. Then, barely two days after obtaining my driver's license we were packed up and heading north to Queensland.

While Mum and Dad were in the Chrysler utility towing the caravan, Wayne and I travelled in the little Singer. It was a long way to travel, and a daunting task for a newly licensed driver. Throughout the long trip our little car wouldn't idle well – it simply conked out if the revs fell too low. Being so inexperienced, I constantly felt anxious. My stomach churning wildly as we drove at a snail's pace up hills behind large semi-trailers, hoping like hell we wouldn't be forced to stop.

Subsequently, my euphoria at finally reaching our destination was short lived! It wasn't long before I realised my life wasn't going to change much at all. In its current state, the dream farm which Dad anticipated would provide us with a living, in fact, couldn't. It seemed that during his inspection, Dad had looked at it through rose tinted glasses. The fact was, many things needed to be done to the property, the first of which was building an irrigation dam, before we could ever anticipate growing a crop. Compounding the issue was the fact that Dad had no real farming knowhow, or rather, he didn't have a clue! He wasn't too far into the venture before he was forced to rethink his ideas.

So now, incredulously; I was being told I was going to be working full time on the farm. Why? I had no experience or desire to do farm work, and it wasn't what I'd envisioned for myself when we came here; I thought I'd finally be a normal teenager and find employment in town. And so, it happened that until Wayne found employment away from home, he and I did the farm work while Dad found employment elsewhere. While we waited to harvest our own crops Wayne and I regularly went out working for other farmers in the area. Every day we'd ride our second-hand pushbikes over corrugated dirt roads to the farms six miles away, or I'd drive the little car up into the hills nearby to pick beans.

For Wayne, who was only fourteen-years old, and me at seventeen, there was very little fun in our lives—none, actually. There were times when

I felt even more lonely and isolated than I had while travelling. At least in the past there was always some form of interaction with other workers during the day. But here I was again being isolated from mainstream society, like Cinderella, but with an evil father and insensitive mother, rather than an evil stepmother. My life was still totally constrained by work, with no real social interaction or opportunities to develop friendships.

The farmhouse was an old Queenslander, situated on the slope of a hill with its back butted into the slope of the ground. The front entry was high off the ground with fifteen steps leading up to the wooden, double front door. It was in a tragically dilapidated and unlivable state when we arrived. Any excitement we might have felt at the thought of finally living in a house dissipated quickly when faced with the reality. The bathroom was unusable, with slippery green moss trailing from the walls and covering the rusted bathtub. Besides trying to get the farm ready for planting crops, the house needed a great deal of repair work done on it before it was livable.

As it transpired, I was the one who was tasked with most of the interior cleaning and painting, and unbelievably, although I was terrified of heights, painting the roof. Wayne had (until he moved away), a bedroom in the house, as did I. Strangely, during the eighteen months we lived there, I never knew the reason Mum and Dad continued sleeping in the caravan. Perhaps it was Dad's idea because after Wayne left it must have pleased Dad greatly that he could creep with impunity in to my room at night.

At fifteen, Wayne's feelings towards Dad were dangerously worrying; Mum feared he'd do something unthinkable. Unknown to me, he had in fact made threats to kill Dad. Believing it would be safer for everyone if Wayne got away from the toxic environment, she found him live-in employment at a bakery in Mooloolaba. I wonder if I'd made that threat instead of simply thinking it, would Mum have whisked me away too?

Wayne and I saw very little of each other for quite a while and I missed him dreadfully. I was totally unaware his threats to harm Dad were the reason he'd left so suddenly, so a big part of me felt angry and to some extent betrayed. Once again, I believed Wayne was given freedom while I continued to be entrapped in an abusive environment. I'm sure I would have felt less resentment if I'd been given the reason for Wayne leaving, especially since whenever I mentioned getting a job in town, I was always told I was needed on the farm.

I remember Mum always having some health issue over the years and during our time in Nambour she had several admissions to hospital. One night during one of her hospital stays, after Wayne had left home, I decided to once again take a stand and refuse Dad's demands to 'be ready tonight.' So, in complete darkness, I crawled under the house as far toward the back as I could, to where the house butted onto the ground, and secreted myself behind a large house stump. Naively, sitting motionless, I didn't for a moment think he'd find me in such a dark and cramped hiding space. Of course, Dad was furious. To my dismay, armed with his powerful torch, he painstaking searched everywhere inside and outside the house and around the yard, calling me repeatedly, eventually finding me in hiding.

To say the outcome was 'as usual' would be to minimise the truth of it. Crawling slowly toward him in the darkness, through the dirt, as he ranted and hurled abuse at me, was a fear-provoking experience. I'd never resorted to such tactics before and his level of anger was scary. Then being subjected to his attempts to kiss and fondle me while he enjoyed my body is an experience I have tried unsuccessfully to erase from my memory.

I felt like a bird trapped in a cage, with its wings flapping but not able to fly, and with no way to escape. I'm not sure how I managed to hang in there while feeling so dejected and powerless until Mum returned home from hospital . Perhaps it was because I was always busy and I really didn't have time to feel sorry for myself. We'd been living in Nambour for over twelve months before I finally found something to look forward to. It was something that would reawaken one dream I'd held on to all my life.

Chapter 19

Can I Hold On To This Dream?

Yes, I had a dream, a passion; a long-held desire to dance. During the itinerant years I'd always felt a natural affinity for rhythm; I'd often dance a little hula or flamenco dance for my friends. That is when I was out of Dad's range. So, when I saw an advertisement for new students at the ballroom dancing studio in town, I thought all my dreams had materialised at once. I naturally felt a mixture of apprehension and optimism, but with Mum's blessing, I enrolled at the Kev Spinaze Ballroom Dance Studio in Nambour.

Kev Spinaze and his wife were Australian Professional Old Time Ballroom Dancing Champions, inspirational both as dancers and teachers. The weekly lessons were a pleasurable respite from my monotonous work and lonely home life. Until Wayne left home, he also attended most classes with me. I seemed to have a natural flair for the Old Time and Latin style of dance, as did Wayne, so we progressed quickly. Those six months I was a student were, until then, the most wonderful period of my life.

Although I was eighteen, I still never received a regular wage or money of my own. This of course meant each week I had to ask for the money to pay for the class. And that didn't come cheaply; there was always Dad's same demand for payment, 'You can have the money if you give me one.' After a while, I got smarter and would wait until Mum was alone during the day before asking her for the money. But unfortunately, attending dance classes meant I needed to borrow the Chrysler, and so ... this elicited another payment.

Any exhilaration I felt after my night of dancing was quickly extinguished the next afternoon when Dad arrived home from work. He'd take great joy in reporting that he'd been told by 'one of the blokes' at work that I'd been seen driving up and down the main street of town the night before. Instead of going to dancing class, I'd been 'hooning' in his Ute. Constantly having to defend myself against such fabrications and undermining rubbish was demoralising. Although Mum didn't believe his story, it did rob me of much of the enjoyment of my dance classes.

When I entered my first ballroom dancing competition, I didn't have any money to buy a glamorous ballroom dress, so I decided to make my own. Although Mum had been a fine dressmaker in her time, having made her own wedding dress among other fashionable outfits for herself and others, she'd lost her confidence over the years and had no interest in teaching me. Wayne, therefore, set about fixing the treadle sewing machine, which the previous owner had left on the property, before instructing me on the finer points of using it.

I'd never sewn anything before, let alone used a sewing machine, so it was a courageous undertaking and a great leap of faith on my part to sew a satin underlay petticoat overlaid with a chiffon outer dress. And may I say in all modestly that I did not look too terribly out of place. To Mum's credit, when I later competed at the Queensland Championships, I had a more suitable ballroom frock to wear. She travelled by train to Brisbane—a long day trip—to purchase some beautiful sequined material which was made up by a local dressmaker. Although the dressmaker didn't have much idea or experience in making ballroom dancing gowns I was happy with the result. And I was very grateful for Mum's effort and believe she really did try to compensate in some way for my hard work.

As our standard improved, we students participated in a number of competitions, where we were moderately successful. I advanced quickly and soon gained my Bronze Medallion. One student couple, who were Queensland Amateur Old Time Open Champions, inspired many of us to emulate their success. As it happened, Kev surprisingly announced that the female partner was leaving in December and offered me her position in the new year, saying he believed I could be Queensland champion within a year. This was what I had been dreaming of all my life, I couldn't wait to get started.

However, I was soon brought back to earth. Mum wasn't moved by my excitement as she had her own unexpected announcement. The farming venture had been a failure so they'd decided to sell up and move to Melbourne. I hadn't seen this coming – I was in shock. I pleaded with her to let me stay in Nambour, saying I could get a job. I could continue dancing. Then the blame game started! Mum said the main reason they were selling was because I'd been having hip problems and wasn't able to do the heavy farm work.

From then on, I was carried along on a tide of disappointment. Once again, I was captive to their control, arrangements had already been made for me to live with our friends in Melbourne until they arrived. Then the even bigger surprise; I was booked in to start a hairdressing course in Melbourne the following year. Once again, my life was in their hands, my dream was shattered. Here I was, within months of turning nineteen, being forced to uproot my life and this time leave the dancing I loved.

Even if I'd had the courage to resist, I knew I had no way of supporting myself. *Would I be able to get a job? What work could I do?* After all, I had no experience to offer. And regardless, after all the years I'd worked, I had no money of my own to start living independently. I had nothing to show for all my years of work. And I felt apprehensive; moving to Melbourne would mean a big life adjustment, life as I knew it would be turned on its head. Just how clueless and unworldly I was would, I knew, become glaringly apparent soon enough. The magnitude of the task ahead was at present only a vague imagining.

I felt heart sick at leaving dancing. And, I was worried. *What would it be like living with people I hardly knew?* Yet, despite that, I felt an underlying sense of relief. Ever the optimist, I could see the positives of my situation might outweigh my fears. Now, finally, I'd actually have some freedom; I'd be a long way from Dad. Why not put the hard work and abuse behind me and embrace the new experiences with gratitude? Who knew what adventures lay ahead, at last I would be able to learn to make my own decisions; I'd be free! And hadn't I always said one day this bad stuff wouldn't be happening!

Ballroom dancing when I was 18, 1963.

Me in 1957. I was 12 and a half years old.

My brother, Wayne (aged two and a half), and me (aged five), 1950.

Part 2

'When you learn to accept instead of expect,
you'll have fewer disappointments.'

— ROBERT FISHER

Chapter 1

Freedom

One moment I'm at the Brisbane airport, the next I'm on my way. I arrived in Melbourne in November 1963; thrust into a new world and a new life. The Melbourne I remembered was still there, only this time I saw it through the eyes of an adult. This, my first foray into taking personal responsibility, was terrifying. I'd spent nineteen years thinking others were responsible for my fate, now, I needed to take on that responsibility myself.

I hardly knew this family so I was naturally apprehensive, nerves fluttering under my ribs as I got ever closer to my destination. Fortunately, it was a relief that this middle age couple with a daughter not much older than me, welcomed me warmly, making the settling-in process seamless. To my great delight, I finally I had a real bedroom of my own; a private space where I could lock the door at night, free from the fear of a nightly visitor.

On arrival, my new hosts house rules were made clear—everyone who lives here has to pull their weight – and you have to find a job. This suited me fine; I wasn't used to siting around doing nothing anyway. The family's love of reading also meant that in my free time I could relax and read to my heart's content, without feeling guilty. Even so, I found it difficult to fully cast off the shackles of guilt when I was 'caught' reading; sitting idly immersed in a book, instead of working productively.

Fortunately, within a few days, and aided by my host, I obtained a nursing assistant position at the nearby hospital. I had very few preconceived ideas or knowledge of what nursing involved, so arriving for my first shift I was full of nervous anticipation. Since there was no individual orientation procedure in place, I was shocked into reality as the senior nurse assigned me my morning duties. 'Please bed-wash the patients down that side of the ward, and I'll do this side. And can you remake the beds while you're at it?' A hot flush crept up my neck to arrive in a prickling sensation on the top of my head, I felt faint! *Oh shit! Bed-wash the patients, and make their beds while they're still in them, how do I do that?*

My stunned expression no doubt revealed my ignorance, highlighting the fact I was clueless and obviously needed help. Fortunately, with the support of the more experienced staff, the learning process was made much easier than I expected. I grew to love interacting with the patients and hearing their life stories. Nursing became a labour of love; I didn't even mind the regular night shifts. The quietness of evening gave me an opportunity to contemplate what my future might hold.

As I reflected on many of the patients' life stories, I began to deliberate on how I could make my own life more meaningful. I knew I couldn't ignore the past, doing so would have been to deny or forget it; to disregard who I was and what I had become. My mission was to discover who I could be. Intuitively I was realising I was meant to experience life, not just live it. I resolved to accept the past with all its disappointments, and to use the strength and optimism that I'd tapped into in the past, to put the hurt behind me, and use it to move me forward into the future. As Mark Mason states in his book, *The Simple Art of Not Giving A F*ck*, 'The more we accept responsibility for our life choices the more power we have over our lives.'

How uncanny is it that we can make these resolutions, then they can be turned inside out without warning? Before I knew it, three months had passed – the farm had been sold and my parents had arrived in Melbourne. And disappointingly, they took it for granted, actually insisting I move back to live with them. Why? By now, Wayne had also moved to Melbourne and was once again working and living independently. Why couldn't I? For three months I'd been earning my own money, enjoying my semi independence and freedom, and I wanted it to continue.

My host family was in a bind. I'm sure if they hadn't felt duty-bound to ask me to leave I might have had the courage to fight harder to stay. Even further disappointment was in store—the caravan was once again parked at the home of our original hosts, Leo and Kath. With a sinking heart I was transported back to 1956 and Leo's attempt to sexually abuse me. I still felt that earlier fear of him – knowing I would be seeing him again as a young woman troubled me. I wondered if he'd be more encouraged now that I was no longer a child?

However, the real blow came when Mum demanded I resign from my nursing position. She wasn't interested in hearing how much I'd grown to love it, or that I'd developed a fondness for the patients and the work and wanted to make nursing my career. Or that I'd earlier been accepted into the next nursing training course after only six weeks on the job. When I'd received this surprising news I'd been flabbergasted because I knew many others had been waiting for the training for well over eighteen months. It was a terrible feeling knowing it was over, all because I didn't have the courage—or know how—to stand up to Mum and refuse.

What could I do? I felt trapped, history was repeating itself and I was once again losing control of my life. Mum's reasoning? She believed nursing would damage my back, and I should remember they'd sold the farm because I had hip problems. At any rate, the subject was not up for discussion—I'd already been enrolled in a hairdressing course.

Approaching matron to resign, I felt foolish and embarrassed. After all, I was a young woman, old enough to make my own decisions, yet here I was giving her Mum's reasons for resigning. Naturally, the matron was disappointed. Like me, she believed I showed a great deal of nursing potential. She said she'd been a hairdresser prior to nursing and assured me it had been harder on her back than nursing. Although I eventually grew to enjoy hairdressing, with it affording me the opportunity to work at home while my children were young, it was never my passion. During the following thirty odd years, while enduring neck, back, leg, and hip pain, bursitis, and tendonitis in my elbow and wrist, I often reflected on matron's words. And, I'm sure I kept many a chiropractor employed.

Chapter 2

Now The Threats Resume

While I waited for my hairdressing course to begin, I was employed as a grader in a stocking factory. It didn't seem logical to me to be leaving nursing—a job I loved—to then work at such a mundane job. It didn't surprise me to subsequently learn my position came about via Leo's influence with the factory manager, a man he'd met through his possum trapping business. As strange and unfair as it may now seem, I just accepted that my wages once again went to my parents.

What was Dads' reception on my return? Well, I wasn't shocked, in fact it was no surprise that he just assumed he'd resume the sexual abuse where he left off. Naturally, I was still very afraid of him and his continual intimidation and threats; I avoided him as much as possible. That worked sometimes, but he was sneaky, and he'd often catch me unawares. I can't say I became brave in those few months away, but a part of me did grow stronger. I was determined to resist his demands and threats—I simply couldn't and wouldn't submit.

When Dad's devious tactics and intimidations failed, he resorted to pleading and acting the victim. He even went so far as to suggest I should offer myself to him, telling me he shouldn't have to ask for 'it.' Once he realised I was unwavering, and with his aspirations thwarted, he grew angry and moody. This was when the psychological and emotional abuse came into play once again, where I was bombarded with self-esteem-destroying negativity.

Around that time, I befriended Robbie, a youth my age, whose family were long-time friends of Leo and Kath. One Sunday, while Dad was out with Leo, Robbie telephoned to invite me out on a date that evening. But, as incredible as it now seems, I actually needed permission. Fortune smiled on me that day, because with Dad being absent Mum couldn't defer to him as she usually did, and wonder of wonders, she agreed I could go.

So, imagine this, my first ever date! Scary stuff! I confess I was a bundle of nerves and my imagination ran riot: *How was I to act? What was I to say?* To my extreme relief, the night turned out to be a happy gathering of friends and family, and I didn't feel too out of my depth. In fact, our date went so well, we planned to go out the following Wednesday night. My pleasure was soon replaced by apprehension; my instinct warning me there would be repercussions. I was in for a far bigger shock than I expected.

What transpired when Dad arrived home and heard I was out with a boy was insane. He went half-crazy with rage, making outrageous claims about Robbie. He sat on the caravan steps ranting and raving, repeatedly telling Mum I was in danger. He claimed Leo told him that when Robbie doesn't get what he wants from a girl, he dumps her in the bush. I knew what Dad was about and resolutely put his negative allegations out of my mind and looked forward to Wednesday night. However, what followed a few days later had a profound effect on us all; Dad's deceitful and pathological actions set in motion events that changed our family dynamics forever.

Chapter 3

A Total Betrayal

I'd been working at the stocking factory for some weeks, and although I missed nursing, I was happy and was quite enjoying the job. My function was to grade stockings for flaws or ladders, one stocking at a time. While not difficult, it did require intense concentration. To ensure our nails were kept buffed to avoid snaring the stockings during the grading process, we were provided with hand cream and nail files at each workstation. I thought this was a great perk; for the first time ever, I had lovely manicured fingernails. And once again I was enjoying the company of girls my age – our breaks were full of fun and laughter.

I'd recently received good reviews from the supervisor, so I was surprised and confused when, on Tuesday afternoon, I was asked to report to the manager's office. I approached the office, frantically trying to think of anything I might have done wrong. On entering, I was rendered speechless. There before me sat Dad, the last person I expected to see, looking very serious and important. The manager wasted no time on preliminaries and simply said, 'You need to leave immediately; your mother is ill, and your father says you're needed at home.'

I was almost speechless with shock and disbelief, and embarrassingly close to tears. Mum was fine when I left for work that morning – there was no indication of illness. Gathering my wits, I said I knew two days' notice was required but the manager waved this aside saying under the circumstances he'd overlook this rule. I was completely taken aback by the suddenness of it all and sadly didn't even have an opportunity to say goodbye to my new friends; I simply gathered my handbag and was whisked away.

It had all happened so unexpectedly. I was in a state of complete bewilderment as we walked from the building. My gut instinct, and the sinking feeling in my chest, told me something was wrong with this story; I smelled a rat, it just didn't make sense. Sure, Mum had always been a rather sickly person, but I'd never known her to succumb to an illness this quickly. And, I'd never had to take care of her when she was ill! Dad remained silent and hard-faced as he strode ahead of me out of the factory. Then, as we rounded the corner into the side street, I was dumbfounded. There, in its full glory, was the vehicle with the caravan hooked on behind it, with Mum sitting up in the passenger seat, smiling happily.

'We're on our way to Mildura for Easter,' she said, 'Dad is taking us up to get settled in today, then he'll be coming back with Wayne on Thursday night.'

What the hell was going on? Now feeling wretched and confused, with me once again sitting between them, we drove away in silence. As we headed out of Melbourne, it become clear to me how easily it had been for him to pull the wool over Mum's eyes. How easily she'd been duped. But, it was such a sudden decision on his part; surely she must have questioned why, three days before Easter, he would decide to drive us 300miles/480kms to Redcliffs, settle us in to the caravan park, then return to Melbourne. Yes, he was the master manipulator, he'd snatched back control, leaving me feeling undermined and betrayed.

I felt shattered; this was too much for me to bear; it was the final straw. I realised beyond a shadow of a doubt his reason for doing this. He knew about my upcoming date with Robbie—he was making sure it didn't happen. Mum couldn't understand why I looked so miserable. She was genuinely happy to be on holiday, with the thought of the four of us enjoying Easter together, away from the city. I've no idea what he'd told her about me leaving the job, she seemed totally oblivious to what had just transpired.

As Dad drove away that day to return to Melbourne, I went into total melt down on the caravan floor, letting all my years of built-up pain, fear, hurt, and details of my sexual abuse pour forth. Everything I was feeling was released that day, erupting in a torrent of anger and anguish; I couldn't hold back. Screaming out how over the years he had threatened to blow my brains out if I ever told anyone about his abuse, I unburdened myself of his devious betrayal. In my outpouring of anguish, I even revealed that I knew Wayne and I were adopted, and how Dad had taunted me with it. I was too hurt and disconsolate that day to ask why she hadn't believed me when I was ten years old. As I poured forth my distress, it suddenly dawned that it wasn't about me, it had become all about her.

Of course, Mum was in shock, and understandably hurt and angry at my adoption revelation; it was something she said she'd never intended to tell either Wayne or me. She said she was ashamed that she'd had to adopt when she was able to have children. She then revealed that in the early years of her marriage she'd consulted many doctors and specialists, and after being told there was no reason she couldn't conceive, was advised to seek fertility testing for her husband. It transpired that due to a childhood accident, he was aware he couldn't father a child. How fortunate for him then that it enabled him to abuse me with impunity, knowing he was free of the risk of impregnating me. The ignominy of it was that on many occasions he had cruelly taunted me, laughingly suggesting when my periods were overdue that I might be pregnant.

At the time, it seemed Mum was totally oblivious to my feelings about the abuse I'd experienced. There was no questioning—no searching for details of my experience. Perhaps she heard it all in my rantings. Understandably, she was in shock and pain, yet it seemed to become more about her own pain than mine. Possibly, it was too sudden, too much to take in, in one crazy outburst. As I sat listening to her, all I could think was, *For four years I've kept my knowledge of our adoptions secret so that you wouldn't be hurt.* The pernicious recollection of when I was sixteen flooded in. How, when Wayne and I argued, he'd run to her for comfort, and she'd looked at me with disgust and yelled, 'You're just like your father.' I knew he wasn't my father. And I knew in my heart I wasn't like him. But I couldn't find it in me to hurt her, to tell her I knew, even though it saddened me to think she felt that way about me.

Now the secret was out. Maybe I should have felt some relief, at last I wouldn't have to shoulder the burden of guilt any longer. Now that Mum knew the extent of it, I'd finally have a voice and support for all the emotional and psychological pain I'd experienced. But there was no relief; nothing really changed; nothing was resolved then or later. In fact, now the secret was out, I felt more guilt; more at fault. No matter how I tried to bring it into the conversation over the ensuing years, Mum was resolved in her opinion: I wasn't harmed; it was she who had been betrayed. It was many years later when I was able to open up and seek counselling that I finally saw it for what it was—I was a child and it was the adults who had failed me.

I have no recollection of how we spent that Easter after Dad came back, I've simply blocked it out; but I do remember after we returned to Melbourne the mood was quieter. Nothing was said to me, by either of them, regarding my disclosure. I don't remember Mum shedding any tears for me or giving me any comforting words at the time, either. There was no comforting arm around my body. At any rate, much of what was said that day was blocked out of my mind. There may have been tears other than my angry ones, and Mums' tears in response to the adoption issue, I can't remember. All I know is that I was left feeling even more guilty and it was never discussed again. I heard no more from Robbie. No doubt he'd been understandably embarrassed and humiliated, believing I'd simply stood him up. He was a lovely young man and regretfully I never had the opportunity to apologise and set the record straight.

Chapter 4

The Hostel

Easter was behind me and I was back in Melbourne, ready to start my hairdressing career. Still with my parents, for the first week I travelled to the Academy by train. Thankfully, to her credit, Mum had been working behind the scenes and had finally arranged and paid for my accommodation at the Salvation Army Hostel for Girls in Spring Street, Melbourne. She also paid for the tuition at the Hairdressing Academy, perhaps a compensation for the work I did over the previous seven years. I was grateful she had some insight into my lack of social skills and knowledge of fashion too and enrolled me in to a 20-week deportment course.

When Mum said my hostel address would be kept from Dad for the duration of my stay in Melbourne I was relieved. Perhaps she actually believed me this time. Or perhaps because she failed to discuss the abuse with me, she felt some guilt for having failed to address the sexual abuse years earlier? I was never to know. I continued to worry though; *What if he somehow found out where I was living or sought me out at the Academy?* Not long after it was a great relief to hear Dad had found employment in North Queensland and they'd be leaving Melbourne.

Anyone who lives in Melbourne will attest to the fact the weather is unpredictable. I'd been reminded that four seasons in one day was quite normal when I'd returned some months earlier. When I moved to the hostel in early April, my wardrobe consisted of two summer suits and an assortment of casual clothing that Mum had bought me. Because I'd spent most of my life in work attire, denim and cotton shirts, I was clueless regarding fashion. But, like any normal teenager, I wanted to look good.

Now, here I was in this big city, almost penniless except for the ten shillings/$1 Mum gave me each week, with absolutely no experience in handling or budgeting money. I'd never actually bought any of my own clothes, so I had no idea what anything was worth. And of course, having an almost non-existent sense of fashion, I had no idea what would suit me. As an example of my embryonic fashion appreciation, I wore one regular outfit – bright purple pants, black calf-high boots, and a three-quarter length fake leopard skin coat. Even though I lacked the big city fashion nous, I thought I looked okay.

Part of my problem, even after I began earning money, was that I rarely bought anything, afraid to make a purchase fearing I'd regret it later. Consequently, when I saw something I wanted to buy I'd procrastinate for ages. A fine example of this was my first summer in Melbourne when I had my heart set on a cute bikini I saw on display in a shop window, on my morning walk to work. But, as luck would have it, by the time I finally decided to buy it, it was sold. My hesitation was my undoing, and this experience was a good lesson as it helped me be a little more decisive—'little' being the operative word here—in my future decision making.

There were many nights, sometimes alone, sometimes in the company of other girls from the hostel, that I spent wandering the streets of Melbourne, window shopping and dreaming of all the clothes I'd buy when I had money. The window displays of gloriously colourful fashions were designed to tempt a shopper, and they certainly tempted me. I never tired of looking at the beautiful fashions on display, even though they were beyond my affordability and would be for a very long time.

It wasn't long before I gained a little hairdressing experience and struck it lucky with a Saturday morning job in a salon close to the city. My initial nervousness eventually gave way to enjoyment and the two pounds ($4.00) I earned gave me a much-needed feeling of accomplishment. It also afforded me the ability to buy a few fashionable outfits and an occasional treat.

We hostel boarders were an interesting mix of females of all ages from many different environments. The majority were country girls, many from well-to-do families. Most were in Melbourne studying a trade at one of the many training schools and colleges in the city.

The hostel itself was an old-style five-story brick building, consisting of a variety of room options to accommodate two, three, or four girls. The rooms were lightly cleaned daily and our bottom bed sheet was changed weekly. In summer the hostel roof attracted many of us as it had an interesting view of the city and was a great place to sunbake in private.

The laundry, located five floors down in the basement had drying cabinets lining two walls which were greatly appreciated in the winter, or when the weather was inclement. But the biggest treat in winter was undoubtedly the two baths on each floor. There was always a dash home at night to be there before the rush. We'd fill to the top and then wallow in the hot water. Unfortunately, our soaking time was limited, there was always someone knocking on the door to be next. Eventually, the hot water would run out and a few unfortunates would be forced to wait until it heated up later in the evening.

My roommate, Sandy, was in the same Academy group as me. Our room was long and narrow, our beds set end to end. There was barely standing room between the bed and the dresser set on the opposite wall; certainly not a suitable room for entertaining. We were friends, but not best buddies; no doubt my fault as I'd never previously had a long-term friend. Friendship was made harder because she was from a wealthy family and would spend freely whereas I had to be more frugal.

Sandy was also well-educated, which made me feel inadequate; I seriously lacked self-confidence and self-esteem. Having left school so young, I never felt I measured up intellectually. However, as time went on and some successes came, I gracefully accepted what limitations I had and eventually learned to let go of my illogical belief that I had to be perfect, or as good as everyone else. In the process, I learned to appreciate my strengths and worked on developing the few talents I did possess.

Most of us girls were hairdressing or fashion design students who regularly brought sewing home to complete at night. Because of the poor bedroom lighting, many of them purchased stronger one hundred watt light bulbs to work under at night. They'd use the stronger bulbs while they sewed then remove them before going to bed or the next morning. When they forgot, on their return the next evening, the stronger bulbs would have been replaced with another sixty-watt bulb.

Most of us were in our mid-teens or early twenties, yet despite this we weren't treated as adults. Even though I was nineteen, Mum received a regular conduct report from matron, no doubt because she paid for my accommodation. But the most unpopular rule was the 'no socialising in the common area after 9 pm.' Frequently, as many as fifteen of us would be watching a television program when an officer would walk in at precisely 9 pm and turn it off; no please or thank you, just a 'That's it, times up.' And they rarely relented.

The Salvation Army Officers as a group were mostly kind and thoughtful, although a few failed to display a true Christian ethic. Two particularly, appeared vinegary and intolerant and we, in our youthful wisdom, presumed they were sad bitter spinsters who were lonely and frustrated. They were often rude and intrusive, often eavesdropping on our incoming phone calls. During a call we'd suddenly realise there had been no click when the receiver had been replaced. After we made our caller aware there'd be an audible click. I'm sure it was against hostel policy, but we had no choice but to accept it.

While the strict nightly lockup curfew was not always popular, especially if we were locked out, we accepted it. Doors were closed at 11 pm on weeknights and Sunday and at the stroke of midnight on Saturday. On the appointed hour, the officer on duty rolled down the chain door, directly in front of the heavy wooded double doors situated at the top of the steps. No matter who came along as it descended, it would continue grating downward. The officers were blissfully unaware that the lift light, shining directly in line with the wooden door, would highlight their silhouetted feet where they stood silently, listening as the girls called and pleaded to get in. It made not an iota of difference and many girls were left high and dry, in the cold of night, at the foot of the stairs.

The next afternoon there would be a note on the notice board asking the guilty party to report to matron. Yes, they always knew who was locked out, funny that! It was an inflexible rule, if caught locked out three times, a girl would be asked to leave. That, of course, meant if we were late we wouldn't try to get back in, we'd just make sure we came back next morning during the busy breakfast period when there was less chance of being noticed. As you can see, my life wasn't all doom and gloom. In fact, running the hostel gauntlet at 7 am, especially in a ball gown (yes, I finally bought one), was rather exciting and challenging.

Chapter 5

The Hairdressing Academy

April Fools' Day! Another period of my life had begun. And how ironic that I started my hairdressing career at the Australian Hairdressing Academy, a hairdressing and cosmetology academy, on 1 April 1964. My time at the Academy was to be a very challenging and interesting experience.

In reality, the reason I was here was because two of my older cousins had attended a similar hairdressing college in Melbourne, so Mum in her wisdom decided on a hairdressing career for me. We'd never had a discussion about it as I had felt no desire to be a hairdresser. If Mum had talked to me, she'd have realised I was more inclined toward a teaching or nursing career.

My recent nursing involvement had given me an opportunity to work in a profession I grew to love. It was more suited to my nature of wanting to care for others. So here I was, after seven years working in the fields, embarking on a career which I hadn't really given any thought to. I remember my disappointment that first day when I had to cut my fingernails. After all the years of farm work, of stained hands and chipped nails, I was so proud of the lovely manicured nails I'd groomed and nurtured in the stocking factory. My hair, finally grown to a nice length, got the chop too.

Our unglamorous uniform consisted of a blue, mid-calf length, wrap-around pinafore, belted at the waist with a split peplum collar: a fashionable 1960's style. Our names were embroidered on the front with the academy insignia. This formal style of uniform was designed to give the appearance of style and professionalism. The supervisors wore pink uniforms of a similar style. Male students, a rarity, wore white jackets. Students wore solid white lace-ups shoes with a chunky three-centimeter heel.

In the beginning, much of our time was spent learning the fundamental and practical hairdressing skills by practicing each technique on other students. We'd work in pairs, practicing cutting, perming and setting hair; one being the client in the morning session, the other in the afternoon. The novelty of practicing perms on our hair every day soon wore off; after all I'd been having perms since I was twelve years old. We were always relieved, after a training unit, to progress to the hairdressing salon where we'd work on real clients, who flocked in for the discount hairstyles.

The Academy was a well-oiled operation run by Professor Dibble. We had no idea if he'd been a hairdresser, we only knew he was the principal and if you were called to his office you were definitely in trouble. The second-in-charge, the person responsible for the overall day-to-day happenings, was Miss McKenna. She had the demanding task of organising and ensuring everyone, teachers and students included, were where they were meant to be: at any given time, on any given day. Her duties were time-consuming; not that we students ever acknowledged it!

Our fourteen-and-a-half-month course consisted of monthly intakes of twenty of so students; with one or two teachers, depending on what stage we were at, assigned to each group. The academy was situated in two different premises, one for training, the other a salon taking up two floors in a high-rise building in the middle of the city. Each morning, we'd assemble in our groups and await our teacher's instructions. It was a very comprehensive hands on practical and academic course; we learned everything a salon apprentice learnt in four years, in that fourteen-and-a-half-month period.

Each month, after acquiring certain new skills, we were examined and given an assessment on everything from attitude, attendance, skills, and ability. Parents were sent a report (yes, the hostel matron wasn't the only one to send reports) at the end of each block of training. There was an overarching sense of anxiety and anticipation as the state board examination loomed large at the end of our course – guaranteeing our registration as a hairdresser.

Having said that, Academy life wasn't all work and no play. For some of us more audacious girls, lunchtime meant we could race off to the underground disco a few blocks away to dance the hour away to the latest 60's music, which happened to include the Beatles and Rolling Stones. There were many occasions when we'd only just make it back in time to don our uniforms before the afternoon session started.

Before we knew it, examination day loomed large. Two days of stress and anxiety, consisting of a written and practical examination of all areas of hairdressing, plus facials and manicures. We'd developed the skills from many hours of dedicated hands on experience, so we were certainly ready. Everyone was desperate to pass the first time. However, underlying our confidence was the fear of something going wrong, of not passing an element and being prevented from graduating with our own group. Even a small failure would mean the person had to re-sit that particular element with the next examination group a month later.

As with most exams, there is always the post-mortem; the thoughts of what we might have got wrong, and what we might have done better. The two weeks wait for the final results was a killer. The day the results were released was a celebration to remember for those of us who were successful, and empathy for those who were devastated at missing out.

Mercifully, I'd succeeded – I'd done it – I'd be graduating as a registered hairdresser. Even though I'd done well, I still lacked self-confidence and belief in my hairdressing ability, often feeling out of my depth. It was some time before I actually realised how capable I was. I just needed encouragement and experience in order to continue developing the skills I'd acquired. Within a few short years, I was confident enough to manage salons, my anxiety behind me. With the wisdom of age, I would have liked the opportunity to tell my younger self not to worry so much, not to try so hard to be perfect, to be less self-critical, and to just enjoy the journey.

While I hadn't always been able to display it, I had within me a keen sense of justice and fairness. I'd go into bat for anyone in need, myself included. For years, I had no voice or the ability to stand up for myself, which then affected how I'd react when confronted by what I perceived as injustice. It was after the final exams, two weeks from graduation; I'd hand-delivered a message to a teacher, who'd responded by telling me to, 'Get out,' when I acknowledged a student friend in her class. I immediately reacted, saying, 'Don't tell me to get out,' before turning on my heel and walking away.

Chasing me down the steps and demanding my apology, she then threatened to report me if I refused. Wrong move, lady! Of course, I wouldn't apologise, I told her I would not be spoken to like a dog. The next day, in front of more than eighty students who'd by now heard of the incident, I was, as I had expected, summoned to Professor Dibble's office.

After listening to my side of the story and declaring he could appreciate my point of view, he proposed I apologise anyway, adding, 'You know, I can expel you if I choose to?'

'Yes,' I said, 'I do understand, but I wouldn't apologise to someone who speaks to me with such disrespect.'

When he asked if I could 'try' to apologise, thus giving me an out, I said I would 'try.' Looking each other in the eyes we both knew I wouldn't. Fortunately, I heard nothing further and graduated with my group as expected. The professor no doubt thought it wasn't worth the worry, I'd be gone in two weeks.

Surprisingly, I gave no thought as to what Mum's reaction might be if I'd been expelled. It simply never entered my head to consider the repercussions, this was more about me not tolerating being bullied. I don't know if I learned anything from that experience other than I could stand up for myself when I needed to. Perhaps, if I had replicated that assertiveness in many of my future dealings I would have been better off. Especially where I was to work next.

Chapter 6

Goodbye Melbourne

Now, it was June 1965, with my hairdressing registration papers secure in my possession, I looked toward the next phase of my journey: to find employment. Fortunately, or so it seemed at the time, I was offered a job in a salon in Bundaberg, Queensland. And so, with my meagre possessions stuffed in my suitcase, I departed Melbourne yet again and headed back to Queensland. But, unfortunately, what could have been a positive experience turned out to be another very unhappy period in my life.

For the following seven months, I was employed in a salon managed by my cousin, June, Dad's older brother's daughter. I also shared a flat with her and another hairdresser from the salon. Having never met June before, I felt very much an outsider. It wasn't long before I became aware that she had some of the same insensitive and arrogant traits that Dad and some of his family members possessed.

Cutting unwashed hair was considered normal practice back then: everyone hated it. It was beyond my understanding why June directed every extremely filthy head or any unpopular job my way. I felt vulnerable – my already fragile self-confidence took a beating. Eventually, as a result of the continual disrespect I began suffering terrible anxiety; the pain in my stomach was often so acute, I couldn't stand up straight after working over a client.

When I eventually visited a doctor I spent the first ten minutes of the consultation crying. He was worried about my state of wellbeing, therefore when, a few weeks later the anti-anxiety medications he prescribed weren't helping to alleviate the problem, he suggested I take some time off work. Feeling a failure, and with my self-confidence shrinking more each day, I decided to resign. Later, when I thought back on it, I realised where I went wrong. My inexperience and lack of self-confidence left me wide open to my cousins abuse. I just accepted it because I thought I wasn't good enough.

Foolishly, when I returned to Mackay, instead of taking time to heal, I immediately started job hunting. Within days I was employed in a very prestigious, newly opened salon in the centre of town. The owner, a high-profile Brisbane hairdresser, very up with the latest trends and products, had salons scattered throughout Queensland. Sadly however, I was far from being mentally or emotionally ready; I was, in fact, in a very dark place. Although I continued taking my prescribed medication, I found it difficult to find the courage to go to work.

Adding to my anxiety was once again having to live with Mum and Dad. It was unavoidable. I had nowhere else to go until the rental flat I'd applied for became available. I'd told Mum a little of my experiences in Bundaberg and because she'd had many years dealing with Dad's family and their horrible attitude toward us, she seemed to understand. And since she took medication for her own depression, she seemed to have an understanding of how I was struggling to cope. Naively, I occasionally accepted her medication when she offered it to me.

I was just hanging on by a thread. Sometimes, I broke down during my breaks at work, and I'm ashamed to say I took a tablet one of the other hairdressers offered me. I was really, deeply depressed and spent much of my lunch break in tears. I eventually realised I couldn't continue this way and went to the salon owner to resign. He was surprised and disappointed. He asked me to stay on, saying he believed I had the potential be one of his top hairdressers. Reluctantly, I agreed, but within a few weeks I knew I couldn't carry on. Looking back, I now realise I experienced an emotional breakdown, and I've shut much of that time out; I can recall very little of how I got through it. All I know is that it took a long time before I was able to rebuild my fragile confidence.

Meanwhile, for about twelve months, I'd been keeping company with Richard, a young man I'd met on my first holiday in Mackay the year before. We'd made regular weekend trips to see each other while I worked in Bundaberg. He was attentive and seemed to genuinely care for me; I felt confident our relationship would be long-term. His ongoing support and concern during my breakdown convinced me he loved me.

Within a year Richard's attitude toward me seemed to change. Or perhaps his true colours were showing now that I was in his territory. Our courting wasn't going anywhere; he never took me anywhere special, just an occasional night at the pictures. Often, he'd only call in briefly, usually for sex, always having to rush off for some reason or another. I finally had to accept he'd been cheating on me; for some time, in fact. I was eventually informed that he'd been seeing three other girls while courting me.

This became another rather painful period of my life, another betrayal. Curiously, on one of my occasional visits to see Mum, after I'd moved to my flat, she told me that Dad had seen Richard with other girls in the cafeteria of the drive-in theatre. But, foolishly I'd discounted her words putting it down to Dad being cruel, his wanting to show me that no one would love me as he had always told me.

Even after I became aware Richard had assisted a couple of the girls he'd previously been seeing to obtain backyard abortions, I gave him the benefit of the doubt believing the babies weren't his. He said they were friends he was helping out by arranging abortions and I believed him.

I didn't know how to sever the thread that held me to him. I now see it wasn't love I felt for him, it was more like a fatal attraction. I was only 20 years old and I just didn't believe in myself or love myself enough to see how badly I was being treated. Only in hindsight could I see how I had passed up many opportunities to experience healthy relationships with good men by not opening my eyes to who Richard really was. Only after personally witnessing him out and about with another girl could I accept the truth of it.

I was never one to make snap decisions, in fact, I liked time to ponder a situation. But that very day I made a spur-of-the-moment decision: I was leaving Mackay, there was nothing for me here. I began by making enquiries about work in Mt Isa, but with nothing available I accepted a position in Julia Creek, a small cattle country township, midway between Townsville and Mount Isa in Queensland. Within a few weeks I had resigned my salon management position and left town, leaving few details of where I was going; I just wanted to put it all behind me.

By now it was the height of summer, and I was leaving the sand and surf and cool summer breezes behind and heading west to the wide-open spaces, to country life. On arrival in Julia Creek I was knocked for six by the hot—almost airless—atmosphere that greeted me as I stepped down from the plane. I was told later that the town was six feet below sea level, which resulted in the summers being extremely hot, and the winters, as I was to find out, on the extreme end of the spectrum: bone-chilling god-awful cold.

Julia Creek was amazing! The area was so flat you could see car headlights coming toward you from fifty kilometres away. The first time I experienced this I was truly amazed. We'd been driving twenty minutes after we'd spotted other cars headlights in the distance, before we finally passed them. With its flat wide-open expanses of land, with not a hill— and very few trees—in sight; cattle and sheep grazing contentedly in the paddocks, I was once again transported back to visions of our days of travel throughout the southern states. There was a certain sense of nostalgia for me, and I can say assuredly that Julia Creek was one of my favourite places in Australia.

My employer was a single lady of about thirty, who conducted her business in a big barn-style building on the edge of town. She sold basic women's and menswear, as well as quite an extensive range of men's workwear, manchester, haberdashery, and various household items. My work area was a little room out the back behind the manchester section of the store, where a rather primitive but functional hairdressing salon was set up. It was a wonderful working environment and the clients, especially the male station owners who loved the short back and sides were very grateful to finally have a hairdresser in town. The downside for the salon was that the boiling artesian water flowing from the taps had to be set aside to cool during the day before I could shampoo, or rinse perm solutions from a lady's hair.

Three of us, including my boss and another girl who worked in the local bank lived together in a basic, yet comfortable, two-bedroom self-contained unit attached to the side of the building. It had a pleasant feel about it; a home away from home. However, if we wanted a bath at night, we had to run the water in the morning so it would cool down by evening, similar to the water in the salon. The benefit of being so centrally located also meant we could come and go at will without the need for transport.

The population of the district of Julia Creek, which covered a vast undulating expanse of sheep and cattle stations, was approximately 1000 people. The town was a thriving hive of activity during the week, and weekends brought people together for many social activities in the local hotel and sport club. Although entertainment was minimal, there was a popular outdoor movie theatre, with comfortable canvas deck chairs, where movies were screened almost every weekend. In the colder months, it was fun to sit in the deck chairs, all rugged up with blankets, admiring the myriad stars overhead while watching a movie. The town youth somehow seemed to find plenty to keep themselves entertained and seemed generally happy. In summer, there were many weekends when a group of us drove out of town to water-ski on the lake.

Within a short time, I'd made several new friends and felt I'd been welcomed and accepted into the community. One friend with whom I spent a great deal of time was Aunt Mary, Richard's mother's aunt. She was a beautiful soul, in her nineties, and because of her rheumatoid arthritis was confined to a wheelchair. Aunt Mary lived independently and regularly invited me to dinner. I found her courage inspirational. Despite her disability, she continued doing many things, such as crocheting, most of her own cooking, and housework. She crocheted lovely, lacy, beaded jug covers which I still use more than fifty years on.

As we look back, how many of us might wonder what might have been if we'd made another choice? During my time in Julia Creek I developed a relationship with Arthur, a handsome well-respected young man, an agricultural scientist, whose father owned a sheep station. With time I'm sure our relationship could have developed further, become permanent even. I really loved the open and honest country people and would most likely have stayed indefinitely if not for Richard tracking me down. I'd told both Richard's and my mother where I was going, with instructions he does not contact me; but it seemed he'd persuaded one of them to tell.

When my life was once more regrettably disrupted by Richard, and I felt once more that ill-fated pull, I knew I had to move on. Not because I was going back to Richard, it was more because I realised I couldn't yet reciprocate Arthur's feelings. He'd grown very fond of me and I knew he deserved more than I could give. However, I did not return to Richard in Mackay, but instead headed to Townsville.

Since then, I've come across many young women who've found themselves attached or drawn to certain unhealthy relationships and wondered why! To an outsider, it's plain to see the flaws in such relationships, but for someone who becomes enmeshed in such relationships the struggle to pull away can seem almost impossible. Back then, I had neither the skills nor the role models to emulate or guide me, thus, I floundered on, leaving a trail of heartache behind me. It was a difficult few years, where I struggled to know what love was, and to learn to trust others who professed their love for me. I desperately needed connection, while I continually fought against it, afraid of losing control of my life again. The males I trusted had betrayed me, leaving me unsure of my ability to move on.

After my search for the meaning of my life began, insight came slowly. It took many years of soul searching and self-development work to finally get to a place where I could start to believe in myself – to muster the power to become the person I wanted to be. It was my choice to carry the pain forward or not to carry the pain. I was responsible for my own values of the situation, so if harbouring the pain did not serve me well, then I knew I needed to put it behind me.

Chapter 7

More Goodbyes, Then Townsville

I really don't have any answers for returning to live with Mum and Dad again. Some might think it merely convenience, that I was using them. Perhaps, but I don't think that was the reason, because as strange as it may seem, the need for my mother's love was as strong as ever. Therefore, I found myself, after leaving Julia Creek, travelling to Townsville where she and Dad were living in a caravan park. Naively, I thought I would surprise her, just turn up earlier than I had anticipated and say, 'Hello, I'm here!' Yes, she'd be thrilled to see me! As fate would have it, as I exited the bus that day, who should be at the bus stop but Mum. Oh yes, she was surprised all right: that's an understatement. She was shocked and angry; how could I do such a cruel thing to her, to just turn up without warning?

Why, you might ask, did I keep going back to people who seemed so negative? And after all the abuse? Even to me, it didn't make sense for a long time. The simple answer is I still loved my mother and I wanted her to love me. I needed it! She was all I had! It was many years later, when I worked with broken families and abused children, that I began to understand why I kept trying. In my work, I saw how even though a child was often damaged by its unhealthy and sometimes abusive treatment, when the opportunity was presented to them, the majority of children wanted to return to their mother, to their families. Mother love is a primal thing; it's the love a child finds hard to give up on. And it took a long time before I was able to give up on my need of that love.

It always hurt that Mum saw such negativity in my actions; I hoped she would be excited to see me again. It wasn't as though I was there to sponge off them; I could pay my way. Her problem was simply that I'd arrived without first warning her I was coming. I'm sure she also saw me in a different way now, too. Where once she could drift through life—with no surface issues muddying the waters, pretending all was well—she could now no longer deny her knowledge of what had happened: it was out. After I disclosed my abuse, I believe she saw me as damaged in some way. Although she was still with Dad, her life as she had known it was now changed, and she could no longer pretend it hadn't happened. Her life, like mine, had been to some extent fragmented. It may have been that she continued seeking his love, like I continued to seek hers.

Much to my relief, Dad kept his distance, in fact, he almost ignored me. It seems odd now, but in the beginning, I had no suspicions of what he might be up to now I was out of the picture. Then, when I finally realised he'd befriended a family with a teenage daughter living in the caravan park, I was alarmed. I intuitively knew the intention behind his friendship and felt saddened knowing I couldn't prevent it. After all I had no proof anything was happening, or would happen. Fortunately, within a few weeks I'd found a hairdressing position and was able to remove myself from that toxic environment; I could ignore the uneasy feelings I was experiencing.

Now, I was once again hairdressing and Mary, the salon owner, proved to be a hard taskmaster. She had many innovative hairdressing methods and a huge ego. For the first few months, I wasn't permitted to do much styling as it was her way or no way. I must admit, she was the absolute styling master of long hair and hairpieces. During the eighteen months I worked for her I gained a great deal of confidence as I learned many tricks and methods few other salons were using at the time. Until then, I'd considered myself more of a colourist and style cutter, but now I could add fashion styling to my skill set.

During the 1960's era, a forty-hour week was actually more like fifty hours. Lunch breaks and overtime payments for Saturday and evening work were non-existent and Mary made no concessions for effort. There was no such thing as a lunch break; if someone came in, I'd be expected to leave my lunch and do it. Some days I was so tired at day's end, I'd simply buy a sponge jam roll and a bottle of cream at the local café and eat that for dinner, before falling into bed. At other times, after work, I'd go home to bed, before waking two hours later to have dinner. *Why did I let myself be taken advantage of in this way?* I'm not sure; perhaps it was just how I'd been conditioned , or my belief and acceptance that this was what I deserved.

The one fortunate stroke of luck was finding a share flat with two other girls, just behind the salon. Soon after I moved in, we befriended several soldiers from the Townsville Lavarack Barracks, whose 6th Battalion had only recently returned from fighting in Vietnam. Like us, they were mostly between twenty and twenty-two years old. They were a great group of boys who were lonely for family and considered our flat a home away from home. They'd arrive with their swags on Friday after work and stay until Sunday evening, when they'd return to the barracks. They introduced me to the card game 500 and I loved it. Many times, we start playing on Saturday afternoon and we'd still be playing as the sun rose on Sunday morning.

I was the only girl who developed a relationship with any of the young soldiers. Gary was twenty, a year younger than me, our birthdays a day apart. He was a lovely, kind, sincere young man and we had a lot in common. Our relationship could not be considered easy though, especially for Gary, as my past abuse still troubled me and there was still that pull to Richard, even though we were no longer in a relationship. It was difficult for me to put my heart and soul into Gary's and my relationship; I didn't know how to love, and I just couldn't believe that someone loved me. Despite that, I was happily making new friends and having fun. As usual, when I was content and getting on with my life, as I had been in Julia Creek, Richard would, even though we were no longer in a relationship, drive up to Townsville to visit me. And once again my confusion would rear its ugly head. I've often thought since that time that perhaps he found it as difficult as I did to completely sever the ties.

Life was moving along, and I had settled into a nice routine when Mary asked me to manage the salon for the three weeks while she was on holiday. Gary was on military training at the time so, without a distraction, work utterly consumed my life. It's amazing how, at the time, I thought I was invincible, and foolishly determined to prove I could do the work of two people. Again, my work ethic —or perhaps my ego or pride—wouldn't allow me to refuse anything. I worked tirelessly, and rarely ate a decent meal during those weeks, and consequently paid a heavy price.

Within days of Mary's return, I became gravely ill. The local doctor diagnosed a miscarriage and immediately admitted me to hospital, where I remained for four days. Although I'd had a slight suspicion I was pregnant, I was nonetheless shocked by this bad news. I was so ill and exhausted that I fell asleep and awoke twenty-four hours later. There were other complications which overshadowed the disappointment of the miscarriage, especially with my kidneys. I was in such pain I couldn't travel in a car for many weeks – even walking was difficult. Apart from the body pain, I also lost much of my long hair which to a hairdresser is almost too painful.

After my release from hospital, and because I'd had to relinquish my place in the unit, I spent the next six weeks convalescing with friends. For the first time in my life I was incapacitated; totally helpless and unable to do anything for myself. I remember years later hearing about the many reported cases of soldier's wives having similar pregnancy complications, and speculated if the miscarriage might have been the result of the soldiers being subjected to Agent Orange, a chemical used in Vietnam by the United States military forces.

One evening, during my recovering, Gary surprised me by presenting me with an engagement ring, in front of our friends. Marriage was something I was afraid to contemplate, and it wasn't something we'd ever discussed. In fact, I had no real desire to ever marry; I didn't have the confidence and I didn't believe I could make a husband happy. I had no homemaking skills, I'd never learned to cook, and I didn't want to take on the responsibility of marriage. I was more embarrassed and shocked by his proposal than pleased. I was actually enjoying my freedom; it had certainly taken me long enough to get it. And after all, I was only twenty-two and Gary twenty-one, the last thing either of us needed was marriage, yet I went along with it to save Gary's pride.

No one knew, other than a few close friends, that a miscarriage was the reason for my illness. My recovery was slow and it was more than six weeks before I was well enough to return to work. Being the era before government sickness benefits were available, I had to rely on my savings to get me by. It was disappointing that even though Gary kept Mary up-to-date with my progress, she'd never contacted me personally to see how I was faring. Being the good Catholic that she professed to be, I guess she wouldn't have been too sympathetic toward my pregnancy anyway. In fact, it got back to me on the eve of my eminent return to work that she'd been telling clients I wasn't ill at all. She was a hard and selfish woman and I was now seeing her true colours.

Returning to work for Mary was difficult, and something I didn't look forward to. I'd changed, I guess, with my illness and engagement, Mary's lack of empathy, and my having to make new living arrangements after my six weeks recovery took its toll on me initially. I really didn't have the energy or the inclination to look outside the small square I was in. The accommodation I found though was ideal – a half house with five bedrooms, and only a few hundred metres from the salon. It wasn't long before I was joined by three flat mates. One of these was Sue, a sixteen-year-old who'd just felt the urge to leave home and experience the world. She arrived with a few clothes in a case, a little silky terrier dog, and her sewing machine. This was to be a friendship that has endured for over fifty years. The other two girls, from singleton NSW, were on a working holiday and had recently started working with Sue at the Townsville Telephone Exchange.

Things between Gary and me didn't go too well after that. I confess it was more my fault than his. He loved me too much and I didn't love him enough. Trauma can tend to rear its ugly head at the most surprising of times and Gary's habit of looking at me devotedly, his eyes following my movements, unnerved and angered me. It triggered something within; the memory of Dad's surveillance. There was that fear of losing myself, my control, if I succumbed to marriage. And the fact he was Catholic concerned me even more.

We'd been to see the army priest, who'd declared that although I wasn't required to convert to the religion, any children we had would be Catholic. This worried me a great deal. While growing up, I'd been led to believe that one or more of the children in a catholic family would be required to go in to the priesthood or convent. I dearly wanted children and I couldn't contemplate losing them to the church. I kept my fears and feelings to myself, which I can see now was a big mistake. If I had shared them with Gary, I might have avoided causing a great deal of pain for both of us.

I wasn't happy, but I didn't know why. I was struggling to know myself. I was lost and looking for something, but I didn't know what I was looking for. Reflecting on that time, there was certainly a great deal of disappointment surrounding the loss of the baby. I think perhaps if I hadn't miscarried, things might have been different, I might have been able to settle down and find contentment. As it happened the universe had another path for me to follow.

It was unfortunate that due to my confused state of mind, and not knowing what I wanted or needed, both Gary and I were unhappy; I knew he deserved better! A person can only take so much heartache and wisely he requested and was granted a transfer to the Brisbane army barracks, away from me and my unsettled thoughts.

Chapter 8

Bondi Beach

Life, naturally, had to go on, and although I missed Gary a lot, we didn't really correspond much. I guess we both felt it was best that he got on with life without me, and me without him. Some months after Gary left, Sue and I decided to head to Sydney for five weeks. She travelled down a few days before me while I arranged to spend a few days in Brisbane with Gary, who was living with his mother. We realised the spark between us was still there and hoped we might be able to make another go of our relationship. As he farewelled me in Brisbane, I promised to let him know my decision after my holiday.

On arrival in Sydney, Sue and I found a room in a boarding house in Bondi, home to one of the most famous beaches in Australia, if not the world. We had a fantastic time with a young group of people at the boarding house and the weeks flew by. The weather was hot and Bondi beach was awash with thousands of crazy fun-loving locals and tourists from all over the world. Our suntans developed day by day and we didn't want the holiday to end. The Beatles had just recently brought out their Yellow Submarine album, so we spent a lot of time chilling out on the boarding house lawn, our bodies lathered in oil to enhance our tans ,while listening to the music. It was 1969, well before the 1980 Slip, Slop, Slap campaign alerted us to the cancer risks of sunbaking. It was an idyllic holiday and by the end of the fifth week I'd made the decision to quit my job in Townsville and return to Gary in Brisbane.

However, fate can throw a spanner in the works when you least expect it. With my suitcase packed I was ready to leave when Sue developed a jaw infection and needed medical attention. My departure was put on hold. Sue was only seventeen and I wouldn't think of leaving her alone to recover. As it happened, on a night out at the local hotel with friends a few days later, I met a young soldier on his last night out in Sydney before leaving for Vietnam. He was very like Gary; young, nice looking, and easy to talk to. My memories of the 6th Battalion soldiers on their return from Vietnam made me afraid of what might lie ahead for him. All I can say is an ill-considered one-night stand, based on concern and fear for a soldier's uncertain future, does not a good decision make! I'm not sure why, but as he boarded the boat for Vietnam the next morning with little thought to what lay ahead, we exchanged postal address details.

Later that day, out of the blue, Wayne contacted me to say he was on his way to Red Cliffs, Victoria to pick grapes. He intended staying with Mum's sister Doreen and her family who still lived there. Somehow my fate was sealed, my trip back to Brisbane never eventuated. I contacted Gary and told him I'd decided to accompany Wayne on his trip. With that decision made, Sue and I rang our employers and resigned from our jobs. Sue contacted her brother in Townsville who arranged to collect all our belongings from our flat and take them to Sue's mother's house; and my few possessions to Mum's house in Mackay.

Wayne and I spent the next six weeks working from morning to dusk in the intense Victorian summer heat. While I loved being with my family again, and once more reconnecting with the outdoors, I was actually relieved when the season concluded. The extreme heat was getting to me – I was feeling queasy and out of sorts doing work I was no longer accustomed to. Although I was unsure about my job prospects when I returned to Sydney, I decided I'd face that problem when I got there.

So, with my final grape picking cheque tucked in my bag, I returned to Sydney. By the time I arrived my queasiness hadn't subsided, so suspecting I might be pregnant, I visited a local doctor. Once he'd confirmed the pregnancy he asked when I'd like the procedure? Since I was unmarried, he just assumed I wanted an abortion. After all, it was the 1960's, free love and all that. His response surprised me as I was under the impression abortion was illegal. As I exited the surgery I was, to some extent, in a state of unreality, wondering if refusing the abortion was something I'd later regret. But, like so many times since then, I threw caution to the wind and looked no further than the 'now.'

While I'd been away grape picking, Sue had found a boyfriend who owned a car; so, after telling them my news, and with very little planning and a lot of optimism, we three decided to continue our travels and head further south to Tasmania. Despite our enthusiasm, by the time we arrived in Melbourne, we had barely enough money to pay our passage on the Princess of Tasmania the next day. And, disappointingly, I hadn't been able to cash my grape picking cheque as I'd expected, so we were flat broke; so much so, we slept on the beach in the drizzling rain the night before we boarded the ferry to Devonport.

Obviously, I had no plan regarding this pregnancy, or what I might do in the future. So illogical in hindsight: I had been guiding and advising Sue about unwanted pregnancy and how to avoid it, now here I was, at odds with my own advice. In the past, I had tried taking the contraceptive pill, a few times actually, but unfortunately, I was one of the many women who suffered adverse side effects. I don't think it was confidence that had me accepting that all would be well, I really think it was my deep-seated subconscious desire to have something of my own to love; something that would love me back; something that would make me feel complete; something I'd never as yet experienced.

Chapter 9

Now On To Tasmania

The trip on the ferry over the Tasman that night was nightmarishly rough, with the furious waves throwing themselves over the deck of the ferry in wild abandon. Perhaps they make the trip at night so people can sleep through most of it. When we arrived in Devonport the next morning after a sleepless night, we decided to head straight to Launceston, where we'd heard we'd likely find work. Finally arriving in the late afternoon, our priority was to find accommodation. But after many hours of trawling through real estate offices we soon found, to our dismay, there was no rental accommodation to be had, at any price.

It was mid-March, but we were freezing. It was like mid-winter; the temperature was 0 degrees Celsius/30 degrees Fahrenheit! We'd left Townsville in the middle of summer with clothing so lightweight that layering didn't even work. We were in dire straits when a local man, who'd heard of our crisis, came to our rescue with the offer of a unit. We had no money for upfront rent either, so we were certainly appreciative of this trusting stranger. The unit was gratefully received for sure, but, to us uninitiated Queenslanders, getting the gas heaters to work before we froze solid was a real challenge. Then there was the issue of food. We had no money, so we had nothing to eat! I'd finally deposited my cheque in the bank, but it wouldn't be cleared for five days.

The following morning, Friday, we were out early looking for work, and I was lucky enough to score a senior hairdressing position, in one of the larger salons in the city, starting the next morning. Our next challenge was to try to convince the local shopkeeper to give us food on credit until I was paid for my Saturday morning work. Fortunately, I had a lovely marquisate watch, which I offered to the shopkeeper to hold as security until I returned with some money the next day. Surprisingly, he accepted. Looking back, I'm surprised at our audacity, or was it naivety? After meeting such a trusting landlord we were even more relieved and grateful at having met such a generous shopkeeper.

I'd previously worked in salons with four or five girls, and at the academy with hundreds, but the staff in this salon took the prize for unfriendliness. The salon was owned by a German couple, who, with their daughter, were all hairdressers. Twenty girls were employed permanently in the salon. Like the academy, each senior had to supply their own equipment, which meant outlaying much of my first few weeks wages on hairdressing gear. Another feature was that each senior was allotted an apprentice to work exclusively with them.

Sue—who was employed as a receptionist at the salon—and I were both surprised by their negative attitude, neither of us had ever experienced such antagonism from work colleagues before. During the three months we were there, no one willingly befriended or assisted either of us. I even found that my apprentice was ignoring my instructions and intentionally trying to sabotage my work. Part of the problem may have been that we were both very friendly, and the owners accepted us too well – and we were from the mainland. At the time there was an unfair perception that workers from the mainland were 'up themselves,' considering themselves in some way better.

The male owner Mr. E, as he was called, turned out to be a lecherous individual who should have known better than to produce a pack of pornographic photos to show Sue and me. We were both disgusted, neither of us had seen this type of thing before. It seemed as he got to know us, he assumed we'd be open to his sordid behaviour. I couldn't believe how I seemed to be a magnet for horrid, older men. I certainly didn't enjoy the salon environment, especially after Sue left for Burnie, but it was a job and being pregnant it was crucial that I work for as long as I could.

At first, being aware that pregnancy didn't prevent a hairdresser from working I didn't disclose my pregnancy. I attended regular health checks at the local hospital and during one visit the doctor asked if the baby's father knew of the pregnancy. I said no he didn't, and I didn't intend telling him; it was my mistake not his. Understandably, by now he'd stopped writing. I accepted this, after all we hadn't been a couple and it would have been almost impossible for us to try to develop a relationship with him overseas. And anyway, after only one night, we knew nothing about each other. However, the doctor insisted he had a right to know, so, against my better judgment, I wrote to him. The fact I didn't hear back didn't concern me; I accepted this was my journey and I would handle whatever lay ahead.

That's not to say I took this situation lightly, I didn't! Perhaps my desire to have someone to love, as I'd never felt loved, overshadowed my reality. Only time would tell how real life was to become. I had no previous experience with babies or children, so I knew I was going to need all the courage I could muster to get through the challenges that would no doubt be thrust upon me in the future.

Then, as the southern winter blizzards descended with a vengeance, the Asian flu virus arrived on the scene. People were being encouraged to have the flu vaccination, especially pregnant women and the elderly. Unfortunately, this meant I was obliged to disclose my pregnancy to the salon owners earlier that I intended. Mr. E. didn't accept it well, and of course didn't believe my story of a husband in Vietnam. It wasn't long after that, when I was four and a half months pregnant and hadn't even begun to show a bump yet, he asked me to leave due to my pregnancy, and within the next few weeks if possible. I felt shattered, because I knew looking for another position at this stage of pregnancy was practically impossible. Once more, I was set adrift on an ocean of doubt, wondering not for the first time what I'd gotten myself in to.

Chapter 10

My Forced Return North

Fortunately, I was still close to Richard's mother in Mackay so when I rang and told her about my situation she contacted her friend, who owned a salon, who willingly offered me a position. It was a tremendous relief to know I could continue working until my baby was due. However, the journey back to Mackay was a major undertaking over four long and uncomfortable days of travel. The first part of the trip was once again on the Princess of Tasmania, another rough and wild night's journey across the Tasman. I couldn't afford a berth so sat up all night in the recliner seat, not the most comfortable way to travel while pregnant.

The one exciting aspect of the trip happened just after we left Devonport, when I experienced my first baby movement: a short jolt. It was something I didn't know about or expect to happen. It was exciting, my baby became a real entity, a life, and I spent the next few hours unsuccessfully pushing my stomach trying to feel more bumps.

After spending the day in Melbourne, I boarded the Greyhound coach at 9pm for the trip back to Mackay. The first twenty-four hours were a nightmare. Here I was, in the middle of winter, on a coach with air-conditioning problems, the vent under my seat spewing out freezing air instead of warm. Sleep was impossible and luckily, after the first night and day, the coach driver, realising I was suffering from the cold apologetically offered me the drivers bunk up the back of the coach. When I arrived in Mackay four days later, I was barefoot; my feet and ankles so swollen I couldn't get my boots on.

Mum, by now, alone in her little one-bedroom cottage after Dad finally abandoned her for his latest woman, didn't actually throw down the welcome mat on my return. And although I had let her know I was coming, I hadn't mentioned my pregnancy. As it happened, Mum still had the caravan parked beside the house and reluctantly agreed to rent it to me. I felt uncomfortable being there knowing how Mum felt about me and I'm sure I would never have returned if things had worked out differently in Tasmania.

However, the reality was I was back, and this created other problems, especially for Mum. So, in order to make it easier for Mum to face her friends and family, I agreed to say my husband was a soldier in Vietnam, who I eventually lost in the war. Having had to live with too many secrets and lies already, I found this difficult. Having been brought up being told a liar is worse that a thief, here I was lying to the whole world. Another secret, so hard to keep tucked away from view, another to add to the long list I already harboured.

Mum, of course, didn't believe I'd told the baby's father about my pregnancy, or that he hadn't replied. To appease her, I wrote again, this time asking him to acknowledge my letter. I said if I hadn't heard from him in the next few months, I'd contact his mother, whose address I had, to ask after his welfare. I made no claims on him, I merely said the doctor believed it was my duty to tell him. This time I did receive a reply telling me to never contact him again and to leave his mother out of it. Well, I had the answer Mum wanted, didn't I!

Looking back on that period of my life, I really do wonder what my relationship with Mum was about. What lessons, if any, were we learning from each other? Why was I continually being drawn back, time after time? Was I unconsciously torturing her, bringing more heartache each time I returned? I can only say I'm sorry I was such a disappointment to her when all I wanted was to love her and her to love me in return.

Mum had her own demons, hurts, and fears like everyone else but at that time I was not mature or wise enough to understand. I'm sure she did the best she knew how and would do much of it differently if she had the chance. I've blamed both my parents for some of the things that happened in my life and judged them both by focusing on their weaknesses and defects. Perhaps I could have focused more of the positives, especially Mum's, if I had not been so affected by the negatives.

I'd like to say I've always been a good person and a good daughter, but even though I know I've tried to be, there have been times where I've felt I've failed miserably. I know through my thoughtlessness and, some might think, selfishness, I put Mum through some hard times. It seems I was the base of much of her heartache, starting with her adopting me at such a mature age, the sexual abuse, and now being an unwed mother. To someone bought up in such a strict, puritanical Methodist world, I must have seemed a totally flawed individual.

Chapter 11

1969 – My New Baby Boy

Back in Mackay, I was once again working in a busy salon, this time with thirteen girls. I worked full time up until a month before my due date, then part-time until a fortnight before Craig was born on November 1st 1969. The salon atmosphere was great; a far cry from the Launceston experience. Everyone was welcoming and excited about my baby being a part of the salon family.

Up until I had Craig, I really didn't have a great deal of confidence in my mothering ability, and sincerely wondered if I could be a good mother. My confidence was given a great boost by the midwife who thought I'd had lots of experience; I was a natural, she said. In all honesty, I was totally in love with my baby boy thinking surely he must be the most beautiful blue-eyed baby ever born. He was born with a soft down of brown hair, which soon fell out to be replaced with a head of almost invisible snow-white hair. During the following three and a half months I was amazed at how much I enjoyed motherhood.

The time flew by and after three months my savings ran out, and I needed to return to work. I never asked Mum for financial assistance—I never would—to then be obligated to her. As it happened, I had a set of very expensive Rena Ware saucepans I'd purchased the year before, and which were still in their original packaging. As much as I hated to part with them, I sold them for half the original price, so I could have another two weeks at home with my baby.

I returned to work on a part-time basis, and when Craig was six months old, I resumed full time work. Luckily, I was able to enroll Craig in the day care centre close to my work. I was fortunate when my single mother status became known to the director, and she provided me with a discount, which helped significantly. Mum had naturally grown fond of Craig and asked if she could look after him while I worked. Although I was reluctant, he was doing well at the day care centre, I agreed, for Mum's sake. I thought this could be good for her, something to take her mind off herself. Thus, we agreed I'd pay her the day care centre fee. I also paid Mum extra for Craig's food and the formula he needed each day. Because of this new care arrangement, I moved out of the caravan onto to the small sleepout inside Mums house so she'd have easy access to Craig's cot during the day. I continued to pay rent and prepare my own food as I had while living in the caravan.

Life went well for a few months, I was enjoying my dual role of work and motherhood. The problem, though, was that Mum insisted Craig have two long sleeps daily, which resulted in him wanting to play at night. By the time he was twelve months old, I was exhausted and could barely function. And, I'd recently become very worried about Mum's capacity to care for Craig adequately during the day. I knew she took Valium, Mogodon, and other assorted medications and I began to wonder if she made him have two sleeps during the day because she was wanted to sleep too.

Unfortunately, on one of my infrequent days off, my fears were confirmed. After hearing I'd planned an outing with a friend, Mum began accusing me of taking advantage of her, saying she only received ten cents an hour for looking after Craig. She became irrational when I reminded her that she had agreed to the day care fee. Accusing me of being an unfit mother, perhaps because I had been seeing a young man at the time, she grabbed Craig from me and ran into her bedroom and locked me out. Frantic with worry, and fearing she'd give Craig a Valium or some other drug, I banged on the door and demanded she come out. When she finally did, I took Craig from her, telling her to never do this again. Becoming enraged, and despite me holding Craig in my arms, she started screaming and punching me.

As I've mentioned, I rarely made snap decisions, but fear for my child that day propelled me out the door. I felt gutted, I couldn't believe Mum could do this to me, or to Craig. As I grabbed my bag and some of Craig's things and headed out the door, I was crying, at the same time trying to calm Craig's frightened cries. I dropped Craig off at the day care centre and headed to the salon because I knew my boss and her husband managed boarding houses and would help me. Within a few hours, I'd obtained accommodation, borrowed a utility, returned to Mum's home to collect all my belongings, and moved out.

It took some time before it dawned on me that Mum had wanted Craig for herself; to replace her beloved son, Wayne. I understood that love, but her mental instability scared the hell out of me. I feared what could happen to Craig if she was drugged up when I wasn't there? Had she made him sleep during the day because she needed to sleep? Despite this, I've often wondered how leaving so suddenly, and not seeing her for many months, might have affected Craig somehow. I guess I'll never know. I'm also sure our leaving, then not having any contact for months, would have hurt Mum deeply. There was never any apology from her regarding her behaviour that day as no doubt she believed it was my fault. Like everything else in our relationship, it was never spoken of again.

Craig's and my new home was an old, yet comfortable Queenslander which had been converted into a boarding house. It was very basic, with a large, central, combined lounge/dining room, surrounded by eight small rooms; a few occupied by tenants. There was a communal bathroom, kitchen at the back, and an open-air laundry underneath the house. After a few months of living in one room, I was able to move into another double room with a stove and sink, so I was pretty much self-sufficient. Another tenant, a kind older lady, often baby-sat Craig when I wanted a night out.

I was fortunate to have a very generous boss, one of only a few people who knew my true circumstances. She lent me a sewing machine which meant I could reduce my expenses by making Craig's and my own clothes. Because Craig was finely built, pants and shorts his size weren't available in the shops, thus I was able to make everything he needed. I made Craig many cotton seersucker shirts in every colour available, which, with his snow-white hair and blue eyes looked very striking.

When Craig was eighteen months old I met my future husband. He was from Sydney and on a working holiday. He was good looking and charming, and I confess to being impressed by his Ford Fairmont car. He was kind to Craig too, which was important to me. He was a car salesman and had various jobs in and around Mackay until he found construction work at the Peak Downs Mine south west of Mackay. After about a year we decided we could afford to move in to a two-bedroom unit together not far from the boarding house, which worked out well as I was able to continue walking to work, pushing Craig in the stroller.

Craig was generally very healthy but often suffered bouts of tonsillitis, and too often needed antibiotics. It was commonplace for me to hear from the day care staff that he had become ill during the day. Eventually, at two years of age, an ear nose and throat specialist advised surgery to remove his tonsils; and adenoids which were so enlarged they'd closed the nasal passages. In the early 1970's, hospitals didn't permit parents to stay with their children under any circumstances. It was heart wrenching to leave my baby all alone, standing up in the cot crying for me as I walked from the ward. I too cried many tears that day.

I guess as parents, not many of us get through our child's life without a few dramas along the way. On one frightening occasion, the young childcare assistant rushed in to the salon screaming, 'Come quickly, Craig's sick.' As we approached the centre I was confronted by the director holding Craig in her arms while he alternated between lying limp one moment and then shaking and screaming the next. I had no idea what was happening, I was terrified! The director simply shoved him at me saying you need to take him to a doctor. Frantic with worry, I ran up the street with my screaming baby in my arms, looking for the nearest doctor's surgery. As we waited in reception the horror of it continued to unfold while I didn't have a clue what was happening.

Craig, I was told, had experienced a convulsion, brought on by a high temperature. After a night in hospital, the doctor said he believed Craig was an overactive child; he'd apparently been running wildly around the ward that morning. He then prescribed phenobarbital medication, which he said would help prevent further convulsions. I was confused, I had no idea what this medication was; there was no internet or google to search for information back then. And of course, doctors were demigods who gave us very little information, but who we trusted to know what was best for us.

I confess, to my shame, I did medicate Craig for some time after; that is, until I realised it was curbing his spirit and discontinued it. The guilt of giving my child such medication even for a short time played on my mind for many years. Had there been some residual effect, how would I know? I was realising this parenting thing certainly brought many challenges, and this I was to find out, was certainly not going to be the last one.

Chapter 12

Sydney / Moranbah 1973-1981

Just before Craig's third birthday, in October 1972, I got married. Wanting more children had played a large part in my decision to marry. It was a simple low-key affair with just family and a few friends but disappointingly, the studio photos which we awaited eagerly never eventuated, it seemed the photographer didn't have film in his camera. Life just continued as before, and within a month, exciting news; I was pregnant.

I'd finished working at the salon before we married, and although the mines were not hiring immediately, my husband sent an application to the Peak Downs coal mine near Moranbah, 200 kilometres south-west of Mackay. Meanwhile, he was offered a car sales job in Sydney, which we felt would be a good work opportunity while we waited. So, with our few possessions bundled into the car we said farewell to Mackay and headed south to Sydney.

We were feeling optimistic and ready for a new adventure. But, we were unprepared for the stressful and disappointing dramas that unfolded as we got under way. No longer driving the flash car, my husband had bought a cheap car before we were married, which we prayed would get us to our destination. Unfortunately, by the time we got to Newcastle, with over one hundred kilometres to go, the car, chronically ill by now, finally gave up the ghost. We were eventually saved by our friend, who drove up from Sydney to rescue us. Our gravely ill car, when finally transported down to Sydney, was deemed beyond resuscitation.

Even though we spent three months living with my in-laws, we were looking forward to finding a place of our own before the baby was born. I was enjoying living in Sydney and felt relieved we'd have family living close by when the baby arrived. Then, surprisingly, we received news that the mine application had been approved. So, within a week, we'd purchased another vehicle and set out once again for the north.

Moranbah, at that time, was not too well established and the population still minimal. We soon realised life in this small township had very little going for it, socially. The Peak Downs and Goonyella Mine companies were progressively constructing houses in the town, which they rented to the miners at a minimal cost. However, due to the long waiting list, we weren't fortunate in obtaining a property immediately on arrival. Although there were numerous houses in every stage of construction, there was no definitive timeframe of when one would be available.

I was seven and a half months pregnant by this time and Craig was three and a half years old. We'd secured a suitable rental house in North Mackay and decided to stay put until the Moranbah house was available. The house was dirty and run down so I set to cleaning it from top to bottom before I felt happy to bring my new baby home. I spent hours those first few weeks climbing up on chairs, washing and scrubbing walls, before I was happy with it. Yes, I must have been a little crazy doing stuff like this in such a late stage of pregnancy. At any rate, my efforts paid off; the house looked and smelled great and I settled in for the few months ahead.

Life sure can throw some curve balls. Just three weeks before my baby daughter was due, the renting agent notified us the owners wanted to return to live in the property. We were given a month's notice. This was before the days of a signed lease, so we weren't in a position to argue our dire situation. What made it even more stressful was the fact that alternative rental properties in Mackay were non-existent, and accommodation in Moranbah was many months off.

Word of our desperate situation soon got around and one of the workers offered to rent us his caravan until our house allocation. With the baby's arrival less than two weeks away, we moved it in to the Moranbah caravan park, thinking we might only be there for a matter of weeks. We were to find out that just because we wished it to be didn't mean it would be so. The caravan park was full of people living in a similar situation to us. As the weeks turned in to months, we always felt a sense of relief when someone received their home allocation: we were then one step closer to ours.

For me, it was particularly stressful, because at that time Moranbah didn't have a maternity facility at the new hospital. Women needed to travel over two hours to Mackay to deliver their baby. It was commonplace to hear of a woman giving birth in the ambulance on her way to Mackay, or the occasional roadside delivery in a car.

Because my due date was only ten days away when we moved out to Moranbah, we decided, rather than take the risk, it might be best to return to Mackay a week prior to my due date, just to be sure. A wise decision as it turned out, as Petah was born four days early, on the day we had originally planned to travel in to await her birth.

Although the caravan was a reasonable size, living in it was not a novelty for me. I'd spent the best part of my youth living in caravans, annexes, and tents; it held no fascination for me at all. The interior consisted of a cooking facility in the centre, a double bed on one end, and a single bed across the front end, which could be made up after the table had been put down at night. Craig slept here, and Petah slept in a bassinet at the foot of his bed. Fortunately, Craig was a good sleeper, because Petah was a restless baby who would continually wake herself, day and night, each time she touched the side of the bassinet. For the six months we lived in the caravan, neither she nor I slept well. Six months in a bassinet was not an ideal bed for a restless and screaming baby.

Those first months were difficult, yet we managed to survive and really appreciated our home when we finally moved in. Unfortunately, Moranbah didn't have a shopping centre so everything we needed, including furniture and food necessities, had to be sourced from Mackay. We were grateful that we were able to buy some second-hand furniture locally rather that travel to Mackay. Before we purchased a cot, Petah slept on a mattress on the floor inside a playpen. That first night in the house I woke at Petah's feed time in a panic. She hadn't already woken up screaming as she usually did so I frantically rushed in and shook her awake fearing she had died in her sleep. It took weeks before I could relax, knowing she could now sleep undisturbed.

Within weeks of moving into the house, I found out I was pregnant again. Although unplanned, it was exciting news brought about by my ignorance regarding taking the contraceptive pill after ceasing breast feeding. The local childcare nurse had told me that because Petah was only putting on two or three ounces per week, my breast milk wasn't nourishing her. I was surprised and disappointed, as Petah was a chubby baby who at 8 pounds 9 ounces at birth appeared to me to be doing well. As it turned out, baby formula wasn't what it was cracked up to be, with the result that Petah simply continued to gain the two or three ounces per week.

The clinic sister failed to advise me about what form of contraceptive I needed after ceasing breast feeding. I naively believed that I needed to start menstruating before I could begin taking the contraceptive pill. Nevertheless, I was happy. I certainly wanted more children, but probably not quite so soon. Just as we were getting our lives and the house sorted out, things took a turn for the worse. Probably the reason I didn't realise I was pregnant earlier was because I hadn't developed any of the normal body changes of pregnancy.

Nine weeks into the pregnancy, I began to bleed. The local doctor, a locum, advised a week of bedrest fearing the possibility of a miscarriage. It was a very difficult time for us; being so isolated; having a six-month-old baby and a four-year-old; and having no family support. We were fortunate, though, to have befriended a young couple while living at the caravan park, who agreed to look after Craig and Petah during the day. My husband, who'd never done any of our washing, washed Petah's nappies in the twin tub washing machine after work. We had to laugh some days later when he said he'd been washing them, not realising they needed to be rinsed in the second tub.

At the end of the week of bedrest, there being no improvement in my situation, I was referred to a gynecologist in Mackay. As he handed me the referral letter, the locum doctor looked at me dismissively and said, 'And don't come back here.' I was taken aback and disappointed at his insensitive attitude; our regular doctor was always kind and caring. When I got home,

I opened the referral letter. Who doesn't? His comment: 'Inevitable abortion'—he believed I was going to miscarry.

Subsequently, I was admitted to the Mackay Base Hospital for what turned out to be ten long days. Lying in hospital feeling unsure what the outcome would be was difficult. Craig and I had never been apart and I missed him dreadfully. However, the true reality of my situation hit me like a brick when, after a week in hospital, when my children came to see me, and my beautiful seven-month-old baby girl didn't seem to know me.

After my discharge from hospital, I'd arranged to stay with friends, who had a baby daughter Petah's age., The Queensland wet season arrived with a vengeance. Heavy rain always brought with it a high risk of being stranded on the Moranbah side of Nebo Creek, midway between Moranbah and Mackay. Many of the other creeks on the highway were also flooded became impassable for days. To avoid the risk, my husband organised to bring the children in to Mackay on Friday after work, to be with me during my recuperation.

Fortunately, he got through as the floodwaters rose behind him. He was quietly congratulating himself until he discovered, when Petah needed a nappy change, that in his rush to get away he'd left her nappies at home. No disposable nappies then, so it was an interesting few days with two seven-month-old babies in one set of toweling nappies. Sadly, for me, it took some time for Petah to reconnect and bond with me after my two weeks absence.

Unbelievably, within a day of leaving the hospital, my body changes began almost immediately, and it was as though this had never happened. Whatever had caused me to bleed for over a month had been a mystery, even to the doctors. This just happens sometimes, they said, and the pregnancy would go ahead without any further issues.

Adam was born 8lb 10oz on Aug 31st 1974, two hours before Father's Day. He, like Petah, was a chubby baby, who fed and slept well, and it seemed that my early health scare had no impact on him. I was relieved and grateful, as subconsciously I had feared he may have issues caused by the threatened miscarriage. Petah was not yet thirteen months old and only walked solo the day I came home from hospital.

I feel blessed that Petah was such a dear little girl: sociable and talkative, saying her first word, puppy, at seven and a half months. As she grew older she continued talking non-stop and entertaining anyone who would listen. While I breast fed Adam, she'd sit on my other knee and cuddle into us. If Adam needed a nappy change, she'd toddle up the hallway and fetch a fresh one. As Adam grew older and began crawling, Petah became like a little mother, opening doors for him to climb into cupboards and generally being the organiser. Then there were other times when she was happy to just sit on the front balcony and watch the world go by. I think she was happy to have some alone time to think about what she'd talk about next.

Craig started Year 1 the following year. It was a busy time organising the two little ones, both in nappies, mealtimes and day time sleeps while slowly developing a hairdressing clientele working at home during school hours. Life was generally happy although my instinct told me there was something wrong with Adam's eyes. He couldn't focus on my face when I was feeding him, and his eyes tended to jump about. I was sure he had vision problems. After visiting Mum on one of our trips to town, she agreed there was definitely something wrong. As my concerns grew, our local doctor referred him to an ophthalmologist in Townsville. So, with Adam now seven months old, we began the journey of unfolding the mystery of his vision impairment. And what a journey it became; and in many ways, for both of us, a lonely one.

Chapter 13

Our Lonely Journey Begins

The ophthalmologist Adam was referred to was regarded as one of the top ophthalmologists in Queensland, so I felt confident that he'd be able to get to the bottom of Adam's problem. I'd like to say our first visit was a positive experience, but it wasn't. Here I was with my beautiful baby boy, all alone in the doctor's surgery, getting a diagnosis I found totally confusing and distressing. Your baby will need surgery the doctor said; he has in medical terms strabismus, an alternated squint.

He explained that strabismus primarily occurs because the two eyes cannot work in tandem. Our eyes generally work as a team, fixing on an object and sending two slightly different signals to the brain. The brain then combines those signals and produces a 3D image: this creates depth perception. When those two signals are out of alignment, the brain can't combine them to form a single 3D image. The result is two misaligned images: double vision. It's like watching a 3D movie without a set of 3D glasses. Combining the images effectively is something that must be learned after birth.

When double vision occurs, the brain sends new signals to the eyes to change alignment to bring the image together. If the person has difficulty doing that, then sometimes they figure out (subconsciously) how to move the images further apart so that the double vision is also further apart and less confusing. This happens by one eye fixating on the real target and the other eye moving in, out, up, down, or diagonally. In most cases, the person becomes very consistent in what they are doing, resulting in a crossed eye or wandering eye, and in Adam's case an alternated squint.

Most surgical approaches focus only on repositioning the eye muscles, assuming if you operate on the eye muscles, you'll improve the alignment of the eyes. Although Strabismus surgery does alter the physical appearance of the eyes, at least initially, it does not solve the problem of poor binocular vision. Even though the eyes often look more aligned, most of the time the person still does not have depth perception or true binocular vision.

While the prospect of corrective surgery for Adam's strabismus was a potential positive, he was dished out a further blow that day; something I'd never heard of before, and it was something surgery couldn't fix.

Chapter 14

Ocular Albinism

Your son Adam also has Ocular Albinism. As simple as that. But, hang on. I'd seen albino children around locally and what the doctor was telling me didn't make sense. These children had white hair and almost transparent skin. Adam wasn't like that, he had normal skin and hair – there had to be a mistake. He couldn't be an albino.

But, unlike today, where computers and the internet give us easy access to information within minutes, in 1975, information was almost non-existent. And the ophthalmologist failed to tell me it was a genetic disorder, or if he did, I felt too shocked and dejected for it to register. If it had been explained, we might have been more prepared for what lay ahead and what was to be a confusing and frustrating period for our family.

It was a lonely journey, living in a mining town; not knowing who to turn to; what help I needed; or where I could find it if I did know. The fact is, I didn't know the questions to ask to get the answers I needed, I just did the best I could. Consequently, I suffered a great deal of guilt because of my ignorance of the true reason for Adam's disorder. Initially, I believed it may have been the result of my threatened miscarriage. Or perhaps it was the pressure on his brain when, at birth, the membrane holding the fluid sack would not break, which meant a long labour. It ate at me and I secretly blamed myself. And of course, as it turned out, I was to blame!

I can't understand why the ophthalmologist didn't explain it more clearly. Adam was fourteen before we had genetic testing to determine conclusively that it was a hereditary disorder. When I was eventually able to do some research, I found out that Ocular Albinism is a genetic disorder characterised by vision abnormalities present at birth in affected males. Although ocular albinism primarily affects pigment production in the eyes, fortunately those affected have normal skin and hair pigmentation. A male has one X chromosome and if he inherits an X chromosome that contains a disease gene, he will develop the disease. Males with X-linked disorders pass the diseased gene to all of their daughters, who will be carriers. A male cannot pass an X-linked gene to his sons because males always pass their Y chromosome instead of their X chromosome to male offspring.

Female carriers of an X-linked disorder have a 25% chance with each pregnancy to have a carrier daughter like themselves, a 25% chance to have a non-carrier daughter, a 25% chance to have a son affected with the disease, and a 25% chance to have an unaffected son. I had two sons; one with the disease, one without; so what were the odds of my daughter being a carrier.

Fortunately, while Craig was not afflicted by Ocular Albinism, he nonetheless had been afflicted with colour blindness, another genetic disorder passed on from me. Vision in humans is made possible by a light-sensing sheet of cells at the back of the eye called the retina. The surface of the retina is populated by specialised sensory cells, known as rods and cones. The rod cells detect very dim light, while the cones are less sensitive to light but are used to detect colour. Together, the rods and cones gather the information needed to create a picture that is then transmitted to the brain.

Colour blindness primarily afflicts males, because the genes for red and green cones are on the X chromosome, and males have only one copy of this chromosome.

Craig's colour blindness was not diagnosed until he was six years old when at the end of Grade one, I was informed he failed math's. He was subsequently diagnosed as being deficient in all colours; it is little wonder he was unable to do simple math using the coloured rods of the math curriculum at the time. Females, on the other hand, have a second X chromosome that serves as a backup if something goes wrong with the first. What a legacy to pass on!

Chapter 15

Our Long Journey Days

Each trip Adam and I made to the ophthalmologist was a marathon effort. Starting at seven months, we made that trip to Townsville, he and I, every three months until he was two-and-a-half years old. We'd set off from Moranbah in the early hours of the morning to drive 200 kilometres to Mackay, where we'd board a flight to Townsville in North Queensland.

Until Adam was eighteen months old, we'd spend a night in a Townsville hotel before flying home the next day. I always took enough toweling nappies for two days, bringing the soiled nappies back securely packed in the bag. From eighteen months it became a one-day trip as I'd make his ophthalmology appointment for around midday, which allowed us to catch the return flight back to Mackay that afternoon. We'd then make the 200 kilometres journey home: they were long days.

Leading up to his strabismus surgery Adam had one eye patched or day per week, a procedure designed to strengthen the muscles around eyes. Because he always pulled the patch off, I created splints for his out of a large polystyrene beer cooler. With his arms in splints and h covered with a bandage he resembled a car crash victim.

When Adam was eighteen months old, I too had issues which attention. I was suffering a great deal of foot pain; a feeling akin on sharp knives which radiated from under the ball of my foot, i It was hard to locate the origin of the problem and I regularly practic treatment hoping to alleviate the pain. Eventually, in went to the doctor. I thought that complaining about my t taken seriously. However, he immediately diagnosed a Morton's neuroma, a growth on the nerve junction between the toes, which required surgery.

So here I was with my youngest child only eighteen months old and needing constant care; a two-and-a-half-year old; and a five-year old at school, and me booked for foot surgery. Following a few days in hospital, a few weeks on crutches, and many months of recovery, my optimism returned. However, I learned a powerful lesson on my return home. Be very wary of obstacles on the floor when using crutches. In one moment of inattention my crutch slipped on one such obstacle and to steady myself I instinctively placed the wounded foot down hard. The pain was so intense I was grateful no one was there to witness my screams and groans. A hard lesson but one well learned in preparation for my future surgery.

Until he turned two, Adam also suffered recurring monthly ear infections, the first at two weeks of age. Over time, he grew so accustomed to them he rarely complained. It was only when he overslept his afternoon nap that I'd check and notice puss leaking from his ear. Because of this, a few days before he was due to have strabismus surgery, I took him to the doctors to get the all clear. A few days later, for the first time, we boarded a small six-seater plane in Moranbah and flew direct to Townsville. As we exited the plane in Townsville, Adam started pulling at his ear, a sure indicator of trouble. I prayed it was simply the air pressure in the small plane but as luck would have it, during the hospital admission check-in he was found to have a temperature and an inflamed ear. Disappointingly, the surgery was cancelled, and we returned home that afternoon.

Adam's surgery was postponed indefinitely; we had to get the ear infections under control. At my wits end, I insisted our doctor refer Adam to an ear nose and throat specialist, which meant another plane trip to Townsville. Whilst our doctor had always rejected my requests to put Adam on a long-term course of antibiotics, the Ear, Nose and Throat specialist prescribed a six-month course; in his opinion the most effective course of action. Thankfully, within a few weeks the surgery was rescheduled.

If Adam hadn't been such a good-natured little fellow who took everything in his stride I don't know how I could have managed. These were tiring for both of us. Whilst I respected the doctors view that taking antibiotics long term left children vulnerable to other infections, this worked for Adam. It was a relief that, after having twenty-four ear infections in his two short years, after the extended course of antibiotics, he never again had another.

The day arrived and we once more presented at the hospital. Adam remained in hospital for five days following his surgery, and the image of him on that hospital bed is indelibly imprinted in my mind. I can still see him—tied hand and foot—spread-eagled on the bed, with both eyes totally covered with patches. My heart broke each morning, as when he awoke, I'd hear a plaintiff little voice call, 'Mummy.' They were long days of darkness for Adam; I was so proud of the way he simply lay still and accepted it all. I had no idea if he was asleep or awake most of the time, and while I wasn't permitted to stay at night, I was with him all day.

It was stressful enough sitting beside Adam's bed not knowing whether the surgery had been successful or not, without what happened next. At the end of five days, when we should have been feeling relieved that the worst was behind us, another blow. Adam had suddenly developed a high fever and the hospital staff, thinking it was chicken pox and fearing it would spread throughout the ward, insisted he be discharged immediately. Here I was, with a little two-year old with a fever of 38.8C, his eyes still covered with patches and sunglasses, wretchedly worried at having to make the plane trip back to Mackay.

When we arrived back in Moranbah, after stopping overnight in Mackay, Adam had become very sick. It soon became apparent it wasn't chicken pox, he'd contracted measles—for the second time. With a temperature of 40C by now, we quickly wrapped him in wet towels, my neighbour Margaret, a nursing sister advised this was the hospitals mode of treatment, then lay him under the ceiling fan to help bring down his temperature. Every couple of hours for the next few days, I'd replace the steaming towels from around his body with cool ones.

Considering Adam's recent hospital experience of being tied down on a hospital bed for five days, I wasn't prepared to put him through more hospital trauma. Blessedly, Margaret was able to monitor his progress during the worst times. It was a tough time for the little chap, with his eyes still in the healing process. Within a few weeks he began to get back to his old happy self; especially since the surgery had been a success and both his eyes now focused as one. By the time we'd had Adam's surgery follow up, then his ear nose and throat specialist following up, we'd clocked up five flights to Townsville in seven weeks.

Not long after Adam was back to his old happy self, something happened that no parent wishes to experience. He was out playing with the neighbourhood children when just on dusk I sent Craig to bring him and Petah home. Adam was nowhere to be found and a full-scale search with everyone calling to him was underway. When all avenues had been exhausted and panic was about to descend, one of the children heard a noise coming from inside a refrigerator in the neighbours carport. When we opened it up Adam was purple in the face and was on his last breath. Muddy hand marks streaked the inside of the refrigerator evidence of his attempts to get out. My heart still beats faster when I recall the shock and horror of that day. He'd endured so much already, what now?

Our fly in and out visits to Townsville would continue six-monthly, for another six years. Eventually, the ophthalmologist came to Mackay to conduct a regular clinic, which saved us the air travel. By the time another ophthalmologist finally opened a practice in Mackay, Adam was twelve years old and needed to have further surgery to correct the strabismus. While we thought it would be easier at that age, it turned out to be a frightening and even more painful time for him. Because of his negative reaction to the aesthetic two days post-surgery he was still up on his hand and knees on the bed, dry retching.

I'm extremely proud of the man Adam has become – it has not been an easy journey for him. I'm especially proud knowing that although he deserved special assistance he has never been given any as none was available at the time, and he certainly never sought it. He accepts his life path with grace and gratitude for the gifts he had been granted.

Chapter 16

More Surgery For Me

Not long after Adam's first surgery, life was back on track. Craig was in Grade four, Petah in Grade one, and Adam now wearing glasses at pre-school. My hairdressing was going well, and life was looking positive; everyone was happy and occupied. I was loving the weekly visits to Craig's class, where I conducted craft lessons for the students, and Petah's class for reading. Then, slowly, I began feeling pain when I was playing basketball or squash, in both my feet this time. Although I tried to deny the pain, I finally had to revisit the orthopedic surgeon. This time, I had Morton's neuromas in both feet, one foot having two. So, in my wisdom, I decided that rather than subject my family to two further surgeries I'd have them both done at the same time. It's amazing how naive one can be!

Adam was due to start school early in the year, so I had the surgery in early January, during school holidays. My husband took a few weeks off to care for the children while I was in hospital for a week, and again during my first week out of hospital while I was in a wheelchair, before moving on to crutches. This time I had double the dose of pain I'd had with the first surgery; getting around was absolute hell.

In my haste to return to hairdressing; I discarded the crutches too early in the healing process. Walking incorrectly caused the smaller joints across the top of the foot to become misaligned. After nine months of seeking relief from a physiotherapist, I finally sought the help of an old bush chiropractor, who conducted his business on his front veranda. He'd been referred to me by a rodeo rider friend who had been healed after a accident. Ten minutes in this old chiros' room, with much cracking and twisting, I walked out pain free. Three days later, after nine months of misery believing I would never be able to wear shoes again, I was almost back to normal and life once again had a shine to it.

Chapter 17

A Different Lifestyle, Yet Surprising Opportunities

L ooking back on those early days I remember the Moranbah that first greeted us as unimpressive, socially and culturally. It reminded me too much of the itinerant community of my youth. I once again felt isolated. Miners were considered a different breed of people by many of the city folk, similar to the itinerant seasonal workers. Miners were also thought by some to be too well paid – there was a sense of envy attached.

Our original intention of staying for two years was certainly turned on its head, with the arrival of two small babies in quick succession. I knew I'd either have to join in and participate in what the community offered, or life would become tedious. In hindsight, I realise I got more out of those eight years living in Moranbah than I had before, or did for many years after. Certainly, more than I anticipated.

Before the town developed a fully established shopping centre, we'd drive 200 kilometres to Mackay every six weeks to stock up on groceries and meat. After buying a deep freezer, which most families did, we'd purchase half a beast at the butcher in Mackay and transport it home; then pack it up for the freezer before going to bed. Eventually, this became a day trip with three children in tow. It was a trip fraught with minor dramas. Petah was eight before she stopped being car sick midway to Mackay. There was never any warning, just 'I'm going to be sick'; then the inevitable clean-up and a change of outfit for Petah before we'd be on our way. Strangely, she was never sick on the return journey.

When my two little ones were small, I began playing basketball in the evenings and squash during the day while they were at kindergarten and pre-school. However, there was a downside to the fun of basketball when I banged up a finger or two which prevented me from hairdressing for a few days.

At the ripe old age of thirty-five—I didn't feel it— I was fit and healthy and life was cruising along, so I decided to join the softball club. I didn't have a clue about the game, it was more about just having fun with the other players. Surprisingly, my good eye to hand coordination at squash didn't transfer to the bat and ball. The undying patience of our coach eventually saw me get my act together, and I did improve a little.

To my absolute shock and delight, at the end of the first season I was awarded the Most Improved Player award. I was certainly under no illusion I was a good player by any stretch of the imagination. But, I guess considering the spectacle I made of myself the first time 'at bat,' when after hitting the ball, I ran like hell only to be told I was on the pitcher's plate— not on first base, it might have been a fitting reward. Standing there that day feeling mortified with embarrassment, with two teams and their supporters as witness to my stuff up, certainly tested my character. Obviously, someone thought I'd learned a bit during the season. The one thing I took the most pride in though was, at thirty-five years of age, I could out sprint the fifteen-year-olds.

Life became busy, with my hairdressing during school hours, and the children's and my sporting activities. My husband had no interest in partic-ipating in any of the activities other than watching from the sidelines. The boys played soccer each season and Petah played netball. Petah was also a Brownie, while Craig participated in the Scouts. You'd think I had enough on my plate, but I still had many things I wanted to pursue. When Adam turned five years, we joined them in the Mackay Nippers, thus for the next three summers we made the 200kms return trip from Moranbah to Mackay every Sunday.

Eventually, over time, the mining community provided many creative activities apart from the sport. For example, for a few years, Harry Racine, a much-admired art teacher, travelled out from Mackay every few months to conduct weekend workshops. Harry was a tall, finely-built, evanescent Englishman, who sported a very arty, black, pencil-line moustache. Although in his late sixties, he had a healthy appetite and admiration for us younger women; it was very flattering. He was an outrageous flirt who made the workshops fun with his continual humorous banter and teasing.

We art students were a small group of mothers enjoying a weekend get together while learning the finer points of oil painting. I'm sure Harry never considered any of us a reincarnated Picasso, yet he managed to make us feel we were creating something worthwhile. While none of us aspired to greatness, we were nonetheless modestly proud of our efforts. Some of us were lucky enough to sell one or two of our masterpieces, and maybe they are still hanging on a wall somewhere. Harry often said I showed some talent, but my biggest drawback was that I simply didn't believe it; an ongoing theme in my life. I gave pottery a go for a while too, but like my painting it was simply an outlet for my undeveloped creative urges.

And it was here, in this isolated mining community, that I first began my self-development journey by enrolling in an external correspondence Grade nine course of English and Italian. I fitted the study in between the children's school hours and my hairdressing clients – I loved it. However, eventually, the study proved too difficult: the main factor being a husband who was unsupportive and openly discouraging. He believed I should be satisfied with my hairdressing career and quite frankly I didn't have the will to argue.

Around the same time, I began my solitary spiritual journey by immersing myself in self-help and spiritual-based literature. I'd always had an interest in metaphysical philosophy; I felt somehow, I might get the answers I sought, I might find the meaning of life, the good and the bad of it. And mine in particular.

I began by sending away for a set of four metaphysical books written by Florence Scovel Shinn: *The Game of Life and How to Play It*, *The Secret Door to Success*, *The Power of the Spoken Word*, and *Your Word is your Wand*. Her books are based on biblical stories and a wisdom that can be applied in our own lives each day. I found a great deal of comfort and positivity in many of her wise words. In fact, the following affirmation in 'Your Word is

Your Wand,' has a wisdom that strongly resonated with me. *'There is no loss of memory in Divine Mind, therefore, I recollect everything I should remember, and I forget all that is not for my good.'*

I endeavoured to integrate this into my own life by shutting my earlier experiences away; the ones my soul decided were not in my best interests. Some might say I was in denial, but I believed it served me better to at least try to forgive the past hurts – to try to remember only what was for my good. Florence Scovel Shinn set me on a path of seeking to understand the world and my place in it. Regrettably, although my path of seeking was based on good intentions, I was a long way from enlightenment.

Chapter 18

Goodbye Moranbah

Looking back, I can see there definitely was some denial, at least of what I was feeling – I wasn't happy. Behind the façade of family harmony lay vexations that were at the base of my discontentment; my husband's continued drinking; a constant drain on our finances. Regardless of what shift he was on, he refused to modify his drinking habits; even when it meant spending our last housekeeping dollar. Too often I was hijacked into buying his beer from my meagre earnings set aside for necessities.

He'd been unhappy in his job for some time so after some soul searching he accepted a Real Estate sales position in Mackay. I felt strangely saddened to be leaving Moranbah where I'd created a busy life and made many friends. We'd arrived in Moranbah, three of us in a car, with essentially nothing but our clothes and my sewing machine and left eight years later; a family of five; a Siamese cat; a German Shepherd dog; a removal van full to the hilt; and two vehicles.

I found work in a busy hairdressing salon almost immediately after arriving in Mackay. After working alone for seven years, it felt great to be working with other girls. We were fast getting back on track and the children were loving their new school. Wayne had also just returned to Mackay too so that was another positive.

Thus, I was gob smacked when my husband had the idea of buying a commercial cleaning business he'd listed for sale. An ideal job for Wayne and me he said. His plan? Wayne and I would do the work with him occasionally helping on the weekend, 'if needed.' I said I wasn't interested.

Who knows if it was my past conditioning or plain stupidity, but against my better judgment I gave in. Just further evidence I didn't have

155

the courage to say no and stand firm. I was now working two jobs. Then, unfortunately, within a few months Wayne decided he wanted out thus we were obliged to buy his share. Now we were both working two jobs.

The next five and a half years were some of the most stressful, tiring, and dispiriting years of my life. I'm sure it was only my resilience that got me through. Working seven days a week from 11 pm, sometimes earlier, without a break until after 6 am; and the weekends crazy. Wearily, we'd be driving home as the daylight broke through to light the morning sky: such a beautifully fresh time of morning, when the birds were attacking the berries on the palm trees in the city centre, and world was awakening to the new day.

I could never truly appreciate the beauty of the early dawning sunrise because I'd be thinking of the busy schedule ahead. Our three children each participated in sporting activities after school and on weekends, so my spare time was taken up with balancing act of transporting each of them to their respective sport. Sleeping during the day impossible. During the five or so years, I averaged between four and five hours sleep each day.

I was chronically tired and depressed and in desperation asked the doctor for some sleep medication. Her advice was to give something up, immediately; I was doing too much. My husband dismissed this saying, 'What do you mean you're doing too much?' He had no understanding at all of my complete exhaustion.

I was gradually losing sight of who I was. No matter how hard or how long I worked there never seemed to be enough time for me. If I was unwell, I'd just tune out and work through the pain while my husband remained totally oblivious. Yet, it was not the excessive workload that distressed me the most. What tortured me continuously was having to leave my children at home alone, every night. Although Craig was now in his teens, I felt the responsibility was too much; I was wracked with guilt.

Each morning as I drove over the bridge toward home, I'd scan the sky for signs of smoke or flames in that direction. I felt ashamed – wondering how and why I'd allowed this to happen? My life's ambition was to have children and here I was, every night, leaving them alone. God, how the hell had it come to this? Why couldn't I stand up and address my fears with my husband? Because he was angry, and I knew he'd simply discount my fears.

Chapter 19

Help, I Need Help

Eventually, I lost all joy of life; I was just coasting on autopilot. Then on a bright and sunny Sunday morning, while driving home after doing all the cleaning myself, not for the first time after he'd refused to awaken after a drunken night, it hit me. As I drove over the bridge toward home that morning, feeling totally exhausted and wretched, I thought, *I should just jump over the side and put myself out of my misery.* Oh hell, I really was in trouble!

I'm sure, like many others, I sought the answers to my troubles outside of myself. I started attending the Seventh Day Adventist Church with my children on Saturday morning where I imagined I'd find consolation. I'd finally found the strength to tell my husband I'd no longer be working Saturdays. Yes, he thought I was being selfish, but it was about self-preservation.

But, religion wasn't the answer; being continually reminded what poor, worthless sinners we all were only made my guilt weigh more heavily upon me. One minute being told God is a loving God, then being told he is fearsome, judgmental, vengeful, and punishing, did not offer the comfort I sought. I needed to be uplifted and encouraged rather than have my sins reinforced so harshly.

I'd threatened, on numerous occasions, that if my husband didn't curb his excessive drinking, I'd be leaving. Yet those threats fell on deaf ears. Feeling exhausted and unappreciated, I had no desire for intimacy with a beer-soaked husband. As a result, the more he pressured me for intimacy the more anger I felt. His badgering was a trigger that resurrected past memories of sexual abuse; reawakening my fears, the anger and the helplessness I'd felt. My secret, and the shameful memories which I thought were safely locked away, now taunted me.

I was just hanging on, existing in a sort of limbo, lost in a fog of indecision. I finally sought help through the Family Counselling Service. I'd never disclosed my past to anyone before now; would I be judged? I'd always felt sullied by the sexual abuse – ashamed to admit my body had been invaded in such a way. After a few sessions the counsellor suggested my husband come to a session. She was confident he'd understand my reticence if I explained the reason was about the former abuse. I didn't agree; but, she was the expert so I eventually said okay.

He said very little at the session so I tentatively brought the subject up a few days later asking him how he felt about the abuse. His response? 'It's in the past. Just forget about it and get on with your life.' He simply dismissed it – he showed no acknowledgment or understanding of how his constant badgering and anger resurrected those frightening memories.

Once again I should put the pain behind me – I should get on with my life. Like I'd put the pain away after each visit to Mum during our Moranbah years. When I was unable to tell him, I was crying because of her attitude toward me, and her inability to understand my inner turmoil. The dispassionate way she'd declare 'You've got on with your life – You've got a husband and three lovely children, and lots of friends, I've been worrying all these years and you haven't been harmed at all.' Sure, I'd 'got on with my life,' it was an accusation – she was the victim here. Perhaps, if I had, like Mum, seen a psychologist twenty years earlier I may have avoided the guilt and shame I carried. Rather than applauding my ability to avoid the victim mentality Mum was disparaging of it.

I have to say though I did sometimes wonder if there was in fact something wrong with me. Was I so unimpacted by the abuse that I could live a normal life? Why did others fall into prostitution or drugs when I had managed to live a normal life? What was wrong with me? Why was I able to enjoy normal sexual relations – was I incapable of feeling? Maybe Mum was right, I hadn't been harmed. I've pondered on this from time to time over the years and have concluded that I have a strength and resilience which has been my saviour. I've learned to not dwell on what was out of my control and to be a positive example to others.

People sometimes think if you don't think about the sexual abuse, it will miraculously fade away. Sexual abuse is not like a broken leg. You can't put it in a plaster cast and in six weeks you can walk again. You might try to run and hide from the knock-on effect of sexual abuse, but you can't erase it. The triggers are always lurking. It's always there – the vulnerability – the fear of losing control – the distrust – the memories you can't erase.

How Had I Failed So Badly?

Things didn't change. Once again, I had given in against my will! The impact of the unrelenting pestering was both emotional and psychological. Desperate thoughts from the past resurfaced, *someone please listen to me*. But this time a terrible feeling of desperation overcame me as I pictured myself causing him harm. I knew I was beyond the state of no return: it was time to leave.

Failure! *How had it come to this? How had I made such a botch of it?* I was overwhelmed by feelings of sadness and heartbreak – I couldn't overcome the feeling of guilt and failure. It took time but eventually the weight of self-reproach began to lift as I began to move forward. I believed children need their father in their life so I agreed after three months to a share situation where the children could live with him for the following three months.

As twelve and thirteen-year old's with inadequate supervision from their father, they were having a great time and were reluctant to leave. I felt devastated and powerless to force them. I realised if I wanted to be with my children I'd have to return. On reflection, I can see where I could have and should have done it differently; but I was too afraid of losing them permanently to make demands, I didn't know if I would be successful.

By now we'd finally fulfilled our obligation to the bank – but there was no longer a cleaning business. There was nothing to show for over five years of hard work. If it had only been the business I'd lost I could have accepted it and moved on. But it was what had been lost to me along the way. I'd worked tirelessly in Moranbah to pay half the cost of the block of land we purchased in Mackay. When it was sold at 300% profit, every dollar was absorbed into my husband's financial schemes.

He was a financial planner now, and on his advice I surrendered a tidy insurance policy to invest the money long term. Gone – used to pay our business tax debt. At the end of our relationship I had nothing. All because I didn't believe in myself or respect my own intuition, my inner wisdom. But, life had taught me there will always be challenges to face – and so I knew I'd ride through this storm like I had the others.

I placed blame on my husband for a lot of what happened, but in reality, I have to accept I played my part in it. By constantly accepting that others knew best, never being able to say NO did not serve me well. Trying to be all to all, was not showing wisdom or self-love. While I could blame my sexual abuse conditioning, in truth the blame rested solely with who I was now. I had allowed others to take advantage of me because I failed to realise that I no longer needed to please anyone. I needed to believe in my own wisdom.

I found a great deal of comfort from the meditation group I attended for a number of years. It was a very supportive environment; I felt comforted surrounded by spiritually minded people while I was going through some tough times. One member of the group gave me a good dose of reality by saying 'instead of feeling regretful and bellyaching about it all, be grateful for the freedom and the good in your life.'

I realised then that my life couldn't always be as I would choose. Sometimes fate takes a hand and leads you on another path—a path of discovery—and the journey is often surprising and mind opening. You have to accept you are meant to be on this path at this time, and the purpose of it you may never know. I finally realised if I was serious about moving on with my life, that unworkable part of my past life should now be left behind me. There was no turning back form this, I would seek a divorce.

Sure, I'd married and failed, but I experienced it—the good, and there was a lot of good—and the bad of it. Life had to have some shades of grey or black, and I did appreciate the silver that could shine through. Admittedly, there were times when I questioned what I'd done to deserve this – but then I'd think , maybe this was just another opportunity to learn and grow. Why dwell on the why of it – push it aside and concentrate on the positives. Give gratitude for all the wonderful treasures I had been gifted; My strength to hold fast when life seemed hardest – and gratitude for the gifts of children.

Chapter 21

Love! What Is It?

Much of what my father threw at me that day long ago had some truth in it, but it was thirty-odd years later, after my marriage split-up, that Mum's true feelings toward me were confirmed. It was a hot, humid, summer North Queensland day – I was visiting Mum after her television serials had finished. She'd long ago insisted I not come while her daytime serials were on.

As I left, I usually made a point of saying I love you. Often, I'd lean down and kiss her cheek as she sat ramrod straight and as cold and impassive as a marble statue. Sadly though, she never reciprocated my affectionate overture. Ever!

My visits weren't particularly enjoyable. I'd learned over the years not to tell her anything of consequence. Whatever I said she'd let percolate in her mind—the facts completely misconstrued—to be thrown back at me during my next visit. No amount of argument or entreaty could convince her she'd misinterpreted what I'd said. These visits therefore were more about duty and listening to her regale me with her most recent illness; or hear what a neglectful daughter her neighbours or friends thought I was.

Because we'd never had any significant deep and meaningful conversations about my life, or how I felt about anything she really didn't know me. And I wasn't one to question her about anything, emotional or personal. I accepted Mum's cool and detached attitude toward me even though it saddened me that she couldn't let go of her own pain long enough to meet me halfway.

One fateful afternoon, as I leaned forward to kiss her cheek, I realised the futility of these affectionate overtures. I finally conceded things wouldn't change. But, I'd finally had enough of her snide remarks and guilt trips. As she walked with me to the gate, I looked and wondered at the coldness and aloofness within her. To this day I don't know what possessed me to blurt it out as I did, 'Mum did you ever love me?' Surprisingly, my question didn't seem to shock her at all. She just looked at me in her cold and expressionless way and replied, 'How can you love a child when you get it and it's eighteen months old, and its nature is already formed? Anyway, you were always well fed and clothed, so you have nothing to complain about.'

Although I had no expectation of a particular response from her, this was in reality the last thing I expected to hear. And yes, I was taken aback! She'd always been as subtle as a train smash, but this wasn't just saying something off the cuff, was it? This surely was something that she truly felt and believed. I can't recall my response; what kind of response could I give to this anyway?

Possibly, she wouldn't allow herself to feel or show me love. My mere presence and the issues that had always surrounded me seemed to cause her pain. Yet she was proud of my accomplishments – especially later in life. Perhaps my success was proof that she had done well as a mother. Even though she and my husband both thought I was wasting my time pursuing study, she nonetheless told her friends of my accomplishment. I truly believe much of her resentment toward me was because of my ability to achieve what she had so desperately desired—to naturally bear children.

One might have the impression that Mum was incapable of loving but that wasn't so. Wayne was adopted, only six days old, two years after me – Mum cherished him. Was that why their bond was stronger? Wayne was a beautiful child with a gentle sensitive nature and I loved him too – we adored each other. Regrettably, as he grew older, Dad unceasingly ridiculed and emotionally abused him at every opportunity. I felt protective of Wayne in a big sister way but Dad created a division between mother and son/ father and daughter. He crafted a deceptive front by seeming to give me preferential treatment, while out of sight more sinister things were in play.

I could to some extent understand Mum's bitterness. She'd been denied the love of a young man, because her father for some unknown reason forbade the relationship. It was a cruel twist of fate that this young man later married one of her friends. They had six children while Mum, who wanted a dozen children, eventually married an infertile man who could give her none. She'd wanted to consider artificial insemination, as IVF was called back then, but Dad wouldn't agree. Sadly, Mum never really came to terms with her unfortunate deal. Years later after I'd disclosed knowledge of our adoption she said she'd never intended telling us, she felt ashamed that she'd had to adopt. How sad for both of us that she denied herself the joy of loving me the only daughter she was fated to have.

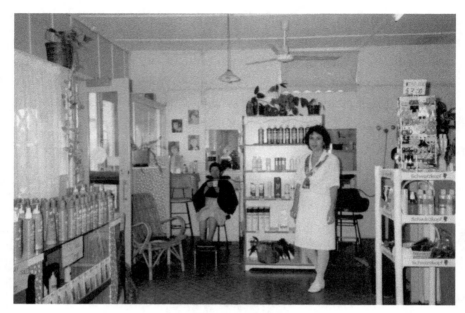

Me hairdressing in Mackay, 1991.

My wedding day, 1972.

Petah, Adam and Craig, 1978.

Part 3

'You can't control the wind, but you can adjust your sails.'

— KRISTEN PROBY: EASY LOVE

Chapter 1

Fight The Fear

'You are not the captive of your past experiences. Here and now you can change what you think, and thus, how you feel.'

— ALBERT ELLIS (PSYCHOLOGIST: RATIONAL EMOTIVE THERAPY)

In his book 'The Slave', Anand Dilvar asks the question, 'What are you a slave to?' Is it childhood wounds or childhood trauma? An unfulfilling or a failed relationship? Or could it be a job you don't like or simply the mundane routine of life? If so, what then does he suggest we do about it?

'Free yourself, and toss the baggage off your back, where you keep your resentment, regrets and guilt. Stop blaming other people and your past for things that don't go right in your life…Your happiness doesn't depend on your parents, your partner, your friends, or your past. It only depends on you.'

He also asks, 'What holds us back?' Is it fear of rejection – of success – of failure – of what people will say – of criticism – of making a mistake – of being alone?' The only thing Dilvar suggests we should be afraid of is not being ourselves, of letting life go by without doing what we want, of failing to take advantage of showing ourselves to other people, to say what we think, to share what we have. No one is keeping record of our failings but ourselves.

Through ideas such as these, I realised I had to let go of my self-doubts and the deep seated fears of my past. Although I did fear rejection, failure, criticism and even success, I knew I needed to recognise my worth and actually start enjoying life. Joining Toastmasters International was my first grand step into taking back control and holding my head high. Through Toastmasters I gradually began to develop a level of confidence I'd never previously had.

For too long I believed I was an uninteresting person with nothing worthwhile to say. But, Toastmasters changed that. I learned ways of telling my story where others listened and I felt heard. As my fears eased, and my confidence grew, I began to see myself in a more positive way. Toastmasters developed my skills to such an extent I was eventually rewarded with a Toastmaster of the Year Award, an Impromptu Speech Award and President of my local Toastmasters Club.

But, deep within me there remained those same uneasy questions – those same insidious fears. Had I actually earned it or was it simply that I was the only person available? Unfortunately, for most of my life, I've fought with that part of my mind which continually questions my worth. The speechless part of me that thinks, *If I can do it then I'm not so special am I – it must have been too easy.*

As it happened though, Toastmasters reawakened my long held academic dream and set in motion my education journey. *Surely,* I thought, *writing speeches must have partially prepared me for writing assignments!* And, hadn't I fantasised about this for years? Here was my chance to prove I was not just a physical or sexual being—this was my chance to show who I really was. My educational journey had been taken from me—now it was time to reclaim it. I didn't need to prove this to the world, I wanted this for *me.* I knew beyond a doubt that I owed it to myself to at least try.

Then in 1991 and 1992 it happened. The possibility became a reality; I enrolled in a night school program and successfully gained credits toward my Senior Certificate.

Oh yes, the studies bug had gripped me – I was excited – what were the possibilities of further study? But what to study? I've always been fascinated by how people think and feel, and the psychology and reasoning behind why humans act the way we do. I finally decided on an discipline where I had personally found help – a field where I might be able to help others; where my people skills and talents could be of benefit. However, I endured a great deal of soul searching before I finally committed myself to an uncertain future. I knew, after my decision was finally made, that only time would tell if I had the necessary strength of character and determination to see my mission through.

Chapter 2

A Mystery Solved – The Missing Link

A part from my commitment to study, 1992 turn out to be an even more significant year—a year of making even bigger decisions. Since Dad's adoption bombshell, I'd continued to wonder about my birth history. In fact, in 1982 I'd attempted a search through Jigsaw, an Australian contact agency for adoptees. Unfortunately, my attempt to find my birth family had been unsuccessful due to my being born in New South Wales, and later being adopted in Queensland. I'd been disappointed to learn that while Queensland adoption records were accessible, the New South Wales adoption contact register was closed – and remained so until 1992.

My enquiry though was more about gaining information about the genetic history behind Adam's ocular albinism, than finding my birth mother. As I intimated elsewhere, I was ambivalent about making contact considering that for most of my life I'd harboured many negative impressions of a mother who could relinquish her baby to an unknown future.

Once the New South Wales restrictive adoption laws were finally relaxed, I obtained my original birth records, which included my mother's full name and address at the time of my birth. Since I now had these details, I decided to conduct my own search starting with the hospital records department. But, disappointingly, I was to learn that all the hospital records had been destroyed in a flood in the 1950's.

Undeterred, I contacted my friend Beryl who was working at the Sydney Telephone Exchange hoping she had access to the telephone records in the mid-1940s to the mid-1950s. I was hoping my birth mother's family had a landline telephone connected during that period. Amazingly, they had, and more amazing still, a member of the extended family was still in residence at the original address.

The prospect of finally making contact was exciting, but at the same time unnerving. I still wasn't clear about my motivation; I wanted to be sure I was in the right mind space – that I was doing this for the right reasons. I deliberated on it for weeks – there was a small part of me that still fostered some antagonism toward my birth mother. However, I needed, and wanted, to know the truth of why I was relinquished, as well as the genetic history behind Adam's Ocular Albinism.

Sue, my friend of twenty-five years, travelled down from Townsville to support me through what we thought would be a long drawn out process of enquiries. But, we were astounded how quickly and easily we made that first contact. Firstly, I rang the female resident at the address and told her I was seeking information about the people whose family tree I was compiling. Surprisingly, she revealed an incredible amount of family history in that one phone call.

I was disappointed to learn though that Dulcie, my birth mother, had passed away seventeen years previously at the age of fifty-two. Luckily, Dulcie's two sisters Freida and Harriette and their brother Joe were still alive. I immediately rang Dulcie's younger sister Freda who was living in Sydney and inexplicably, she wasn't surprised by my call. She said she'd had a strong premonition about six weeks prior urging her to tell my siblings about me and for the past four weeks, she and my younger sister Carolyn had been searching for me through Jigsaw.

I was amazed to learn I had three half-brothers and two half-sisters. Aunt Freda suggested I ring Carolyn who she said would contact the others. I discovered that Carolyn and my other sister Virginia lived in Brisbane, our eldest brother Alvin was living on the Gold Coast, Phillip was in the army and living in Canberra, while my third and youngest brother Terry lived out in Western Queensland. I made it clear that I had no intention of disrupting their lives in any way, promising I'd make no further contact until I heard from them. Although Carolyn promised to pass my details on to my other siblings I didn't want to get over confident.

I was off to night school the following evening so, tongue in cheek, I told Adam 'if any one calls take a message.' In reality I didn't expect to hear from any of them soon, if at all. So, on arriving home that night I was shocked when Adam told me that each of my three brothers had telephoned. It seemed they were actually happy to welcome another sister into their family. It was an awesome feeling knowing I had found a part of the puzzle of who I was.

Since, by sheer coincidence, I was driving to the Gold Coast for a week's holiday with my Sydney friend, Beryl, the following week, arrangements were made for me to visit Alvin at his home. The buildup to the day was nerve wracking. Apprehensively we approached Alvin's door only to find that my middle brother Phillip had flown up from Canberra especially to meet me. Their first words of greeting were 'You're our sister alright.'

It was an amazing first night introduction to my birth family! The boys had generously prepared copies of many generations of family photos which highlighted how different our lives had been. It surprised and pleased us all to see how closely I resembled our mother. I was, however, stunned to find that Phillip, who had very similar facial features to Adam, had Ocular Albinism. I was to discover that by some cruel twist of fate, Dulcie and her two sisters had each born a son who was, to some degree, afflicted with the same genetic disorder.

The weekend? An amazing and thrilling experience, we just clicked. Finally some of my questions had been answered. I was connected to someone by blood. The following New Year I again travelled to the Gold Coast, this time with Petah, to meet up with Alvin and my youngest brother Terry and his family.

I won't stretch the truth by saying I was welcomed wholeheartedly by everyone—I wasn't! Virginia, who is four years younger than me, was suspicious of my motives. Being the middle child of five, and a female to boot, she considered herself the linchpin of the family. Unfortunately, an older sister who her brothers welcomed warmly somehow upset the pecking order. Carolyn was a very sweet person but unfortunately within a few years, we sisters simply drifted apart.

My brothers and I hit it off immediately – we all seem to have the same quick sense of humour. Hearing about their lives growing up certainly made me realise how fortunate I was in many ways, despite the abuse I suffered. Losing the children's father in a motor bike accident when Carolyn was three months old was a tragedy that made life extremely difficult for Dulcie and her children. Never remarrying she reared the children alone with the help of Legacy, an organisation committed to supporting families of incapacitated and deceased veterans. According to Aunt Freda, while the five children were well educated life for Dulcie was difficult. Another mouth to feed, such as myself, would certainly have added to the hardship. Regrettably, Phillip passed away far too young in 2004 at the age of fifty-seven. Although Alvin, Terry, and I live in different states, we remain close.

During our many discussions Aunt Freda spoke often of the true reason for my adoption—or the version the family chose to tell. It seems Dulcie had born Alvin illegitimately in 1943, just after she turned twenty-one and her sister Harriette and her husband looked after him until after the war. In 1944, while working in Brisbane where the American soldiers were based Dulcie became pregnant. I've heard two versions of the story, one that she had been raped by an American soldier; and her brother Joe's version where he stated it had been a consensual relationship. I'm not sure what version is correct; suffice to say Dulcie became pregnant to an American soldier and I was born in early 1945.

I was placed with a foster care family until I was fifteen months old. When Dulcie's man Will returned from the war, they never married as each had married another person to spite the other after a disagreement, they decided to unite the family. Thus Alvin and I were brought to live with them. There is no doubt that it would have been extremely difficult for Will to return from war and be confronted by another man's child, even if she was allegedly the result of a rape. It is a common belief within the family that Alvin was not Will's child either. And I, having been torn from the only home I'd ever known, was reportedly inconsolable.

Will, who was no doubt suffering shell shock—as PTSD was termed back then—unable to deal with my grief tried to drown me in the bath. Dulcie, apparently fearing for my life, and accompanied by Freda, placed me in an orphanage. It seems the reasoning behind her decision was that she was pregnant with Phillip and couldn't leave Will and care for two children while pregnant. Freda said when she and Dulcie returned to the orphanage some months later I had been adopted out. I was 18 months old when adopted.

Hearing that story certainly fitted the missing piece in a puzzle which had plagued and embarrassed me all my life—my absolute dread of saying goodbye—and the teasing that often followed my tears. Now, I saw there was a reason for the sorrow I usually felt when saying goodbye to someone; at least now I understood the deep sadness I'd always experienced with each departure. So many goodbyes in such a short time, at such an early age, left its mark on my psyche.

It's not that I've stopped feeling the loss, it's more about finally having an answer. Knowing why was in some way healing. And learning that my birth mother had returned to the orphanage for me, and had tried for years to find me, was gratifying. I feel a deep compassion for her. I'm sure the pain she felt at losing her daughter was more unbearable each year as she celebrated my brother Terry's birthday five days after mine.

The theories and arguments put forward regarding nature or nurture has always fascinated me. This debate was surprisingly brought to mind when I met my three brothers. Considering I'd planned on entering the Australian defense force when I was seventeen I was astonished to learn that Phillip and Terry had both been in the Army for more than twenty years — and Alvin was in the Navy for many years until he was medically discharged.

I learned that the history of our paternal link reaches back to our four times removed grandfather in 1745. His son, our great-great-grandfather, William, was a convict who was transported from England to Sydney in 1830 for stealing a small oak tree and later a watch. During his many life experiences, he spent time in some of the most horrific and inhumane Australian goals. He was a very intriguing man who married four times, each wife named Mary, three named Mary Ann.

It would be easy to make judgments about him as a person wouldn't it? Yet, as Warren, one of my new-found cousins discovered while undertaking a comprehensive genealogical history of his life speculates; was he an unfortunate innocent, an unscrupulous scoundrel, a hardened convict, or a selfish rogue? We'll never know. However, after reading his story, I wonder; have some of the characteristics I've needed to draw on in my own life: courage, perseverance, determination, strength and the ability to survive life's most unexpected turns, been inherited? Who knows, perhaps it is nature after all.

Chapter 3

I Did It – I'm A University Student

'Success is failure turned inside out—
The silver tint of the clouds of doubt,
And you can never tell just how close you are,
It may be near when it seems so far,
So, stick to the fight when you are hardest hit—
It is when things seem worst that you must not quit.'

DON'T QUIT BY JOHN GREENLEAF WHITTIER

Robert Fisher, in his book, *The Knight in Rusty Armour*, talks about the path of truth, about us; a path we never finish travelling. That accepting the truth about ourselves takes courage. I've spent a great deal of my early life being disappointed in myself; for not becoming something 'worthwhile.' I've had to, as Fisher suggests, accept responsibility for my life, for the influence that people have had on it, and for the events that have shaped it. Sometimes, as Fisher says, 'we have to let go of all we have feared, known and possessed. We need to be willing to embrace the unknown in order to free ourselves of past mistakes and hurts.'

My positive night school experience led me to believe and trust that maybe I could fulfil my educational dream. My biggest challenge was to break through my fear of failure. I had to look within and ask myself, *What is it I want to create and experience for my future? What do I need to do to achieve this*? Once I was able to clarify this my decision was made. I applied to the University of Central Queensland and was accepted into the Bachelor of

Social Science Psychology Degree course. I was 48 years old and about to embrace the unknown.

I had to dig deep and let go of the limiting belief about myself and learn to love and trust my own wisdom and intuition. To let go of my fear, not knowing whether it was a fear of failure, or a fear of succeeding. My rational mind was telling me, *This is what you want and need,* but my irrational mind was saying, *I don't think it's possible.* I don't know if I knew it, or simply wished it, but somehow deep down I had a sense that it was possible.

I know now that we are all born with an inherent faith and trust in ourselves and the future but along the way we can lose this. In his book, *You Were Not Born to Suffer,* Blake D Bauer states, 'When we find the courage to face our fears and go after our dream – take the plunge into unfamiliar terrain, life can become amazing. Once we honour and love ourselves enough to trust our own judgment we are on our way to fulfilling our destiny.'

It is not until we stop compromising ourselves for others love, acceptance, and approval, that we are able to regain the faith and trust in ourselves. I've proved that if the desire to learn is there, all it takes is commitment. That's the great thing about life and the challenges that are thrown our way, we can keep learning and growing and passing on that wisdom – we will never know it all. My marvelous educational journey was not about showing the world I was as good or better than anyone else; it was about trusting my intuition and proving to myself I was capable.

My university voyage was three intensely fulfilling and gratifying years; the first year was spent at the University of Central Queensland, Mackay Campus, now Central Queensland University. Fortunately, I was unaware of what lay ahead, what effort would be required. If I had known, perhaps I may have had reservations about the whole dream.

The reality of what lay ahead began to dawn on me as Orientation day progressed and each lecturer outlined what we faced in the first semester. A one thousand word essay sounded almost unachievable, but when one lecturer announced an essay of three thousand words my heart almost stopped. Then, the bibliography; oh my god, were they speaking another language? Thoughts raced through my mind, *What have I got myself in for?*

But I'd made a commitment and I wasn't about to quit before I started. I'm not a quitter.

How, you might ask, did I expect to actually get through a university course? I'm sure it was the devil in all those positive self-help books I'd been reading that made me do it! I often didn't have a clue what I was doing but I did it anyway and found out that negative experiences were often the best teacher.

This was truly a leap of faith and trust in my own judgment. For starters, my typing experience consisted of a six-night, two-hour course at TAFE, culminating in a grand maximum typing speed of seven words a minute! Is that really called speed? I bought a second-hand computer and an out of date dot printer although my knowledge of computers and printers and their technological enigmas was almost non-existent. I was a hairdresser for goodness sake. I hadn't needed a computer – I could barely turn it on and off.

Initially, I was reluctant to admit my technical ignorance. However, a university community can be very helpful and supportive; or competitive and unsupportive, as I was to find out later. Fortunately, during that first year I was surrounded by many kind and helpful students who willingly came to my aid. I'd regularly turn up at the campus and announce; *'Can anyone tell me which buttons to press to do (whatever the task was) on the computer?'* I'd write the answer in my trusty notebook before heading home to complete the task.

There were times when the task ahead seemed beyond me but I accepted every new skill takes time to master; and I had many skills to master that first year. Things can sometimes go wrong and for me it happened spectacularly. It was near Easter break and all assignments were to be in by Thursday – many of you know that feeling of pressure I'm sure. At seven words a minute I'd worked doggedly all day and well in to the night, on an assignment due the next morning. Too tired at midnight, I decided to print it next morning. But, next morning, on starting the computer, my assignment was nowhere to be seen! Shock, horror, and panic fought with each other as I frantically searched. It was gone! And I had no answers for its disappearance.

How do you tell your lecturer you have lost your essay? It's difficult! Sometimes, the truth can seem stranger than fiction; this was such a situation. Fortunately, maybe because I was a devastated mess, the Chancellor believed me and granted an extension. So, instead of spending the Easter break resting my overloaded brain I rewrote the essay. According to my technically savvy friends, while I had been conscientiously saving my work all day I'd been pressing the wrong two buttons. A hard lesson, well learned!

To compound my mental stress I contracted Ross River Fever mid-year which unfortunately, had been diagnosed as measles. Consequently, I was unnecessarily quarantined at home alone for over a week so I couldn't infect others. I eventually recovered and returned to study, but it had certainly taken its toll.

During that first year at university, I managed to work part time in the salon I'd been managing for five years, while continuing to do my private hairdressing clients at home. The following year I was accepted into the Queensland University of Technology in Brisbane, where I completed my Bachelor of Social Science, Psychology Degree in 1995. While I didn't regret my decision to study in Brisbane, it was heart wrenching leaving Adam behind in Mackay. And of course, my many good friends and clients – almost everything I had known for more than twenty years.

Beginning my second year at a new university was tough. Most students were continuing on after first year – friendships and study groups were already formed. The Psychology Degree, new to QUT, had many students vying for a small number of spots in the honours program. It was a totally different environment, the students here 'knew the system.' I was well into my third year before I finally wizened up to how the system worked.

During my final year at university, Petah, who had left school midway through Year 11, was now 21 years old and enrolled in Year 12 as a mature age student at a Sunshine Coast high school. Returning to study was a challenge for her too and there were many weekends when I travelled up from Brisbane to offer moral support, often bringing assignment information from the university library.

I confess, during my hairdressing years, I was often, to my shame, somewhat disparaging of university students having three months break at the end of each year. I now learned first-hand how, at years end, when everyone is dead tired and just wanting to sleep and not wake up, the stresses of final exams and finalising assignments is overwhelming. As each study year ended, I'd ask myself, '*Can I do this again next year?*'

Petah and I completed our study two days apart; I finalised my final exams on Wednesday, went home and cut out Petah's graduation dress, travelled up to the Sunshine Coast on Thursday, completed sewing her dress on Friday, before styling her hair for her graduation that night. It seemed a fitting celebration for both of our educational endeavours.

Reflecting on my educational journey and what it entailed I'm immensely proud; I proved to myself I could do it – I finally felt I measured up – I could hold my own. And I hadn't given up when times were tough – I'd achieved my dream.

Chapter 4

Now For A Real Job

As my university days faded into the background and the new year dawned my future was uncertain. I was in a kind of limbo – what work was I prepared for? Petah had moved to Brisbane after graduation and had gone to a job interview as a Youth Leader with an after school and recreation association. She happened to mention I'd finished university and was looking for work. Surprisingly, I was invited to attend an interview for the position of Assistant Co-coordinator where I was then offered the Co-Ordinator position.

Although only a part-time position, working with children between the ages of four and thirteen years, it was an enjoyable role which I held for the next three years. Preparing programs and supervising as many as eight youth leaders in the after school and holidays programs was certainly an unfamiliar learning journey. With such a wide range of age groups and personalities there was always something to have a bit of a laugh about at the end of the day. And with so much spare time I had an opportunity to complete a Certificate of Counselling at the Australian College of Applied Psychology.

Working part-time also gave me an opportunity to build a nice little home hairdressing clientele and do some more enjoyable things. For example, I studied Astrology for a few years and found it particularly interesting to incorporate into my counselling knowledge. I also completed a sports massage and aromatherapy course at the Aromatherapy College in Brisbane. After completing my course I was offered a few hours a week assessing and marking course work for the external students. Two mornings a week, I worked at a naturopathic clinic where I did the occasional massage and general reception work. It became a very full program and I absolutely loved it.

Even though I enjoyed the after school/vacation care work, I wanted to broaden my experience and utilise my Psychology knowledge. I was drawn once again to young people and for the next three years worked as a Boarding Supervisor, first for a year at the Koralbyn International School in Beaudesert, an hour's drive south of Brisbane, and then two years at Clayfield College in Brisbane.

As it happened, after five years apart, and many moves for both of us, Petah was finally living back home with me. We were family again, friends and companions. Thus, my decision to accept the boarding supervisor position at the Koralbyn International School was a double edge sword. While I needed the job, I was torn apart; I finally had my daughter back home with me and I was truly happy at last; but now I was once more leaving her behind.

With the dissolution of a marriage, a child's loyalty can be often be torn. Some children can become a pawn, or the go between. Unfortunately, Petah was the middle child – the daughter – the mediator. At fourteen, she hadn't understood that her father's and my needs were no longer the same. While her father wanted to be 'friends,' no doubt hoping I'd change my mind, I needed to move on with my life. Petah wasn't mature enough to understand that by agreeing to go on outings I'd be giving her father false hope. As a consequence Petah felt a great deal of resentment toward me.

And unfortunately, unknown to me, my husband had while inebriated disclosed to both Craig and Petah separately, that he was not Craig's father. Another betrayal. When Sue rang (Petah was living with her in Townsville at the time), to tell me what Petah had revealed to her, I finally understood part of the reason for Petah's resentment toward me. Only after I explained the true and complete story could we re-establish a loving relationship. And yes, I deeply regretted not telling Craig the truth of his parentage when he was younger, but as he grew older he and his father's relationship had been deteriorating and the time never seemed right to discuss such a sensitive subject.

The day I left for Koralbyn was therefore one of the saddest days of my life. The goodbye was terrible – I was a tragic figure as I drove away that day. I'd unfortunately broken my ankle a few days prior to getting the position and was on crutches. Unable to drive my manual car, Craig let me drive his automatic while he drove mine. Stopping on the side of the road midway through the journey I broke down sobbing. I felt my heart would break – I couldn't believe I was leaving my daughter behind.

Chapter 5

The Boarding School Experience

My duties at Koralbyn International School were five days per week from 2.30 pm on Friday until 9.30 am the following Wednesday. I was no longer working with four to twelve-years old. I was now supervising girls from a mix of thirty odd nationalities, many with very few English skills, aged between twelve and twenty-two years. Foremost in their minds, due to the pressure from parents back home, was the need to do well. Convincing Asian students, who were used to studying late in to the night, of the 9.30 pm lights out rule was near impossible.

On Wednesday morning, when I finished my shift, I drove 130 kilometres back to Brisbane to stay with Petah where I still maintained a bedroom. The two mornings I was in Brisbane I continued my receptionist work for the naturopath. Also, wanting to maintain our spiritual meditation practices, my friend Fiona and I formed our own meditation group conducting our weekly Wednesday evening sessions at the naturopathic clinic.

These were very special evenings. Meditation had been my go-to for comfort, when my marriage disintegrated, and later when I was a student. I'd adopted a spiritual mindset with like-minded people and was comforted knowing I could draw on a higher power in times of need. I'd missed it. It was here that my automatic spiritual writings slowly surfaced too, channeling messages of positivity which I shared with the group members.

We all have times in our lives where we use different strategies to deal with life's issues. Where in my youth, I had used stories in books as a way to escape the pain of abuse, now I used meditation to tap in to my inner being, my higher self, and to give thanks for the strength and resilience I've been gifted. When I occasionally feel overwhelmed by life's issues I no longer need to withdraw or block it out – I now meditate to regain the calm.

Little did I know then that the universe had another surprise in store for me – without warning, Koralbyn International School closed down. My beautiful south west Queensland lifestyle experience came to a sudden halt. Most of the students were dispersed to other boarding schools and luckily I almost immediately found similar employment at Clayfield College in Brisbane where I stayed for two years.

Simultaneously another phase in my life was unfolding. My dear friend Sue and I bought a house, on a three-hectare block in the Sunshine Coast Hinterland. The house, surrounded by trees and palms, and a wild disorganised garden of uncontrolled plants and shrubs was a lovely peaceful haven to return to at the end of my four-day shift in Brisbane. Still earning less than a basic wage and paying a car off; I was now committed to paying my share of a mortgage. Once again, I was placing my faith in the universe – I wanted so badly a place to come home to that I looked beyond the risk.

Then, by chance, I met the District Bailiff who was responsible for six Sunshine Coast Magistrates Courts. Within no time I accepted the position of Deputy Bailiff. Not long after I obtained my Commercial License which then enabled me to do private process work. My life took on an extra level of intensity and ambition; on my four days off from the Boarding College, with the Deputy work supplementing my meagre income I succeeded in achieving my dream holidays.

Chapter 6

Moving In Another Direction

Then, once again – that urge for change reared its head. I wanted and needed a greater work challenge. Employment where I could utilise my university degree, one where I could actually contribute in some way. Because I enjoyed working and interacting with others, especially young people, I decided to apply for a position of Child Safety Officer with the Department of Communities.

The universe was on my side once again and after an initial panel interview I was deemed 'suitable' for a position. I soon realised though that being deemed 'suitable' was only the start of the process. Gaining employment in an industry where positions are few and far between, with many only temporary, was tricky.

While it certainly wasn't the standard approach, I called in to the local Department of Communities Centre in my area and asked to speak to the manager. Amazingly, she granted me an interview that same day. Although no positions were available lady luck continued to travel with me. Within two days I received her call. I was offered a six-week locum position that had suddenly become available – but which she could not guarantee would progress to a full-time position.

Instantaneously I was overwhelmed with a feeling of positivity. I accepted the position immediately trusting the universe would take care of the future. As it turned out my trust and faith were validated as six weeks later I was offered a permanent position. Sometimes things are just meant to be as I've discovered throughout my life; when I let go and trust the universe to supply me with what I need, I let good things happen.

The next eight years as a Child Safety Officer were amazing, rewarding, and I admit extremely challenging, but I absolutely loved it. Once again, I was on a steep learning curve and, but for the amazing administration officers, team colleagues and a supportive and inspirational Team Leader, I might have faltered. Unfortunately, there were never enough hours in the day to achieve what I wanted to, but seeing children's lives changed and enhanced was all the reward I needed. At the start, I often felt quite overwhelmed by the task ahead and perhaps it was stubborn pride that kept me focused, and the fact that in the past I've never been one to give in when times get tough. It's amazing what strength we can tap in to when we're tested.

It's not until you enter this field of work that you realise the responsibility you have, making decisions every day to ensure the children have the best care possible. And working with foster carer's, amazing people who give of twenty four hours a day, caring for damaged and vulnerable children. My daily interaction with the many children, carer's and many non-government agencies all working for the welfare of the children, was something I found filled my need to contribute.

At first, I was shocked by the anger and violence of many of the often drug and alcohol affected parents whose children were removed from their care. My first encounter with such a parent left me stunned as I'd never previously been confronted by such anger and abuse. I soon accepted it as part and parcel of the job. Even though my own father had been an angry abusive man he never displayed such anger and vitriol as I experienced in that position. Fortunately, I knew this anger and contempt was directed toward the child protection system and not toward me personally.

When I stopped to consider how I might feel and act under similar circumstances I more easily understood the anguish many of these parents felt. I realised too that the majority of parents we worked with loved their children, a great deal. But, unfortunately, many had had poor, or non-existent parental role models themselves – they simply didn't know how to be good parents. Then there were those who were caught up in the drug and alcohol, or domestic violence scene. No matter the situation it was always sad to see parents and children separated.

Even though I took pleasure in my Child Safety Officer role I still felt a need to pursue other areas of child protection. So, after a period of five years, I took on another challenge – training and supporting foster carers. This too was an extremely gratifying role and it was here that I gained a greater understanding of the motivation behind ordinary average people wanting to foster and support vulnerable and frightened children.

Foster carers are extraordinary people with generous hearts who open up their homes and family life to strict scrutiny in order to fulfil their carer responsibilities. A great deal is expected of them as they perform a job that many could not and would not take on. I feel deeply honoured and grateful to have journeyed along with many of them for that short time both as a Child Safety Officer and a Support Worker.

I loved my work and being part of a unit. Yet, there was one aspect during those first few years, that I found difficult. When working and bonding over sad and often abusive cases one gets to develop a bond of sorts with work colleagues. Unfortunately, because the act of saying goodbye was a dark hole in my psyche, seeing a team member depart would always distress me. People say it shows you care, but to me my over sensitivity meant embarrassment. It's not something I can 'fix,' so rather than actively avoiding closeness with others, over time I've simply learned strategies to help lessen the hurt.

In the past, I know I've bewildered, and no doubt hurt many people, people who genuinely cared about me. I'd just walk away, trying to not look back. I still occasionally struggle with this. I've felt shame and regret and too often left it too late to summon the courage to retrace my steps to reconnect. In the past I've let my irrational fear of rejection just control me. I'd say I don't really care what others think but deep down I knew that wasn't so. Perhaps the real reason, in the past, I didn't let my guard down was if others didn't get to know me, they couldn't judge me.

My retirement from the Department of Communities came without a lot of thought. I'd had another major foot surgery and I'd been on sick leave for six weeks. I felt vulnerable and unsupported by my superior who was critical of my not seeking permission for extended sick leave. While I never expected special treatment, the lack of empathy from my superiors was nonetheless hurtful.

When it was time to say goodbye to my colleagues I realised I had healed much of my fear of goodbyes and for the first time I felt comfortable having a farewell celebration. It was a celebration of connecting with like-minded people who cared about children and worked to make their lives better. Yes, I shed a few tears, but they were happy tears.

I might have retired from my primary full-time job at Communities, but I wasn't idle. I still worked as a Deputy Bailiff and Commercial Agent for Ron for another two years. Knocking on doors and serving people with summons might sound rather unsavoury and unsympathetic but it is non-the-less a very respected and necessary occupation. The early morning starts, and late afternoon and early evenings work finally came to an end when Ron chose to sell his Commercial Investigation business and retire as Court Bailiff. Now, my work life of 55 years had come to an end, I was truly retired.

Chapter 7

The Rewards Of Retirement

Retirement! It has its rewards and I made a promise to myself that on retirement I would now enjoy the fruits of my years of saving and living frugally. I'd realise my childhood dream to travel and see the world and all its wonders. While fulfilling my family responsibilities, and having no personal savings until now, I'd sometimes wondered if my opportunity would ever come. Yet as I watched my single childless friends tripping off to faraway places, I didn't envy them.

Somewhere deep within I kept believing that someday my dream of travel would be fulfilled. Yes, it was a dream, but I truly believed it would come true. I'm so grateful for what I've been able to achieve and experience since those lean days of endlessly trying to make ends meet. Saving the money earned from my second job working for Ron enabled me to have some amazing holidays and make unforgettable memories.

It's almost beyond my comprehension how much travel I have experienced since 2004 when I first joined the Department of Communities. On Ron's and my first trip to war torn East Timor I saw first-hand how war and killing had impacted the country and how lucky I am to live in such a safe and beautiful country. Our 2005 trip to beautiful mountainous and windswept New Zealand to celebrate with Petah and her husband Todd's first wedding anniversary. Then later experiencing the eye-opening trip to Thailand after the Tsunami tore the country apart and witnessing the enormous effort of the people courageously getting their lives back on track. Then later observing the hustle and bustle of Vietnam and Cambodia and learning of the people's sad legacy of the wars and genocide they'd experienced.

My second trip to Europe (I'd spent a month in Germany in 2006), was to attend Craig and Tatjana's medieval inspired wedding with Ron, Petah and Todd in Denmark. The mid-April weather was spectacular, with just the right amount of crispness in the air. The five-hour road trip travelling through the German countryside gloriously awash with golden sunflowers went too quickly.

What a glorious sun kissed day it was for their celebration of love with the bride and groom accompanied by fifteen guests wearing medieval costumes. A lovely civil ceremony and an indoor photography session was followed by a leisurely stroll through the cobblestoned streets of Tonder, then to the park nearby for an outdoor photography session. An authentic medieval style feast, followed by dancing and singing, ended the days celebrations.

After returning to Frankfurt Ron and I flew to Dublin, Ireland where we spent a few days sightseeing before hiring a car and meandering our way through many small towns and villages, on our way to Belfast in the north. We were both smitten by the beauty of the land, and admiring peoples tenacity in enduring their past troubles. Ron returned home leaving me to spend a final week in London with my young German friend as my guide. It's amazing what one can experience in a few short days and I have to confess I loved every minute of the trip. And to be fortunate to see two amazing stage shows 'Wicked' and 'Lord of The Rings' was another dream fulfilled. Only a few years later Ron and I travelled back to Europe to enjoy the beauty of Rome, Florence, Sienna, Venice and the glorious sparkling waters along the Amalfi Coast of Italy.

Yes, dreams can come true, I want you to believe me when I say that! I'm not telling you about these amazing adventures to brag about where I've been but to let you know that if you never give up on your dream, somehow, someday it may come true. It's not by luck I've had these experiences. I've worked hard for a long time, reared a family and for some years was a sole parent, worked two jobs, and done sometimes menial work. I know I've earned it.

I've made promises to myself and I've kept them. One such promise was that when I retired I would use my long service payout to fund an extended holiday overseas. And so, in 2013 it happened! My friend Sue and I embarked on a three-month holiday travelling through Mexico and South America. The absolute joy of visiting Machu Pichu, Peru; Iguassu Falls, Argentina; and the Galapagos Islands were only a few of the multitude of memories indelible. I feel blessed to have had so much history unfold before me on this journey. Suffice to say it would take another book to tell it all.

Then in 2015, at age 70 years, I embarked on an eight-week solo journey through Europe. There was no definitive reason for going solo, it was simply a feeling of just going with the flow and taking one day at a time – without sharing another's agenda or timeline. It was a journey of self-discovery in many ways where I learned how self-reliant I really am. I had only an arrival destination, Amsterdam, and two nights' accommodation booked before I left Australia; and my return plane fare from Paris eight weeks later. I had some idea of a few countries I'd like to visit, but the most exciting part was planning it day by day. How does one describe the exhilaration of hopping on a train in one country and a few hours later arriving in another? In all I visited nine countries, some I hadn't considered, and they were in fact some of the best experiences I had.

My dreams of traveling the world have been fulfilled many times over and my gratitude is immeasurable. I was busy making plans for my second eight weeks solo trip when out of the blue I received news I never ever envisaged receiving. So sadly, that trip was put on hold indefinitely.

Chapter 8

The Worst Possible News

It was 8.30am on Thursday June 9th 2016. Just as I reached for the phone it stopped ringing. Accessing the recorded message I was surprised to hear my doctors soft voice.

'Joileen this is Doctor P; can you please give me a call when you receive this message?'

Puzzled thoughts flashed through my mind. *Why would my doctor be calling me today, especially at this hour in the morning? Surely, she knows I have an appointment to see her on Monday to get my test results.* With a sense of disquiet, I dialed her number and was connected immediately. There was no preliminary chitchat as happens with social calls, she got straight to the point.

'Joileen it's not good news I'm afraid. The test you had on Tuesday has come back. The results are positive, you have breast cancer. I'm sorry to give you this news over the phone but I didn't want you to spend all weekend worrying and waiting until Monday for the results.'

I stood stunned, routed to the spot, momentarily lost for words. It was as though a hot wind gust had brushed across my face and body leaving me weak all over. What to feel? Disbelief? Shock? I just stood, frozen in time, in the centre of the room trying to come to terms with the unreality of it. Yes unreality, this wasn't real! Some moments of blankness passed before I was able to focus on the doctor's words.

'Can you to come in for an appointment, at 1pm today? We need to discuss the test results and your treatment options. It's important we get on to this as soon as possible. Is there someone who can support you?'

'Yes, Ron will come with me. Thanks for calling, we'll see you at 1pm.'

Seriously, I thought as I put down the phone, *thank you? Thank you for telling me I have breast cancer?* What the hell just happened? *But why am I so shocked*, I asked myself? Surely you remember the ultrasound that took forever, then the radiologist performing a mammogram to check the unusual mass on the screen. And then the needle biopsy which really spelt out the possibility of something going on in there! You must have thought this was a possible diagnosis, surely? Yes, but that was a maybe, a possibility, a 'we are just being cautious' kind of thing. But this is reality, this was a definite reality. This is cancer, the big C.

As I surfaced from my daze and walked from the room, I felt the energy drain from my body. A light-headedness surged over me; I wondered what I was supposed to do. Do I cry? Do I scream? What do people do, when they receive this kind of news? This is me. This is real. Why does it seem so unreal? The doctor said the tests were positive. Maybe I'm not in this reality. Maybe I'll come out of this daze and everything will be as it was. Dozens of thoughts rushed and cascaded through my mind as I waited for Ron to come home. *This doesn't mean I'm going to die! I can't die, there is so much more to do! I'm only 71 years old for God's sake! I have grandchildren to see grow up. My children still need me to be here. And I want to be here.*

How long does it take to really assimilate the knowledge that one has cancer I wondered? Maybe I'm not in touch with reality; or maybe they've made a mistake with the results! But first things first! Let's see the doctor, and then look at what options are available. I spent the next few hours before the appointment wracked with anxiety – just long enough for my mind to run riot with a multitude of crazy thoughts. *Oh shit, what do I tell my children? How do I tell them I have cancer?*

Then it was one o'clock. I was still feeling vague and lightheaded, suspended in that unreality zone; this couldn't really be happening! My stomach churned as I sat listening as the doctor read out the biopsy results and outlined my treatment options. And there it was – in her opinion, surgery – chemotherapy – and radiation therapy were inevitable. And it would be best not to delay seeking a specialist opinion.

Things moved quickly, too quickly! Within five minutes my doctor had secured an oncologist appointment for the following day. I felt as if I was being carried along on an outgoing rip tide that I had no way of counteracting. Up till now every day seemed to just come and go at a steady relaxed pace. Now, every thought and action seemed to have an urgency to it; everything seemed to be travelling at breakneck speed.

Following a long sleepless night, Ron and I presented at the oncologist's rooms. As we approached, I wondered absentmindedly why these places seem so quiet and impersonal. And what were the receptionists thinking as we filled in the forms – maybe they don't think anything at all! After all, it's just a job, they see this every day. Fortunately, within minutes the young, attractive female surgeon greeted us. She was calm, unemotional and detached which I guess she needed to be. Thank goodness because I was feeling anxious and thinking, *this is going to be very interesting*!

After studying the ultrasound, mammogram and biopsy result and conducting a physical examination – she presented my treatment options. We're looking at a 19mm mass, so you'll need surgery to remove it. *Ok And!* This mass will be sent off to pathology for tests before we can make any other plans. Hopefully we'll remove the whole tumour, however, if we're unsuccessful, it will require further surgery. As this is a lobular hormonal cancer you may not require chemotherapy, but we can't discount it completely! *Whoa! You won't be putting that shit in my body!*

'Of course,' she continued, 'we won't know until we do the surgery and see what we are faced with. During the surgery, we'll also perform a test to see if the cancer has manifested in the lymph nodes. If this test proves positive, you'll require further surgery to remove those particular affected lymph glands. And of course, after this type of surgery you'll most likely need to have radiation therapy. There is always the possibility of a mastectomy if the result of the initial surgery is not successful.' *There you have it*, I thought, *it doesn't sound too positive to me!*

'When would you be available to do the surgery?' I asked even though I didn't for a minute contemplate going the western medicine surgery route. Not for me the immune destroying chemotherapy injected in to an already weakened system. Or the radiation therapy that burns and destroys the good as well as the cancerous tissue. I had seen first-hand the results of such methods in many women and the long road back from such cures.

'I'll need to consult with the radiologist regarding the radiation therapy and see whether she feels it would be appropriate in your circumstances. We could do the surgery soon; the waiting time is only a week or so. Go home and think about it and I'll see you next week, then we can talk about the options again and finalise a surgery appointment. If you don't get back to me, I'll give you a call in about a week.'

'Think' was the operative word here! All I could do was think. I knew cancer didn't pop up overnight. The cancer research I'd read reported that a cancer took from eight to ten years to grow to the size of a pea. Mine was the size of three peas so I thought this has probably been growing inside me for 25-30 years. I could attest to the fact that cancer didn't mean you felt sick. I was feeling great. In fact this was the best I'd felt in a long time. I'd been watching my diet and lost a few kilos and was planning on taking another long European holiday in a few months' time. All I had to do was book the flight. Well, as they say, 'shit happens!' That trip was certainly on hold now wasn't it!

It's crazy how often after a serious health diagnosis everything quickly evolves into crisis mode. There is this instant sense of panic: to do something now, next week, or soon. But why? Well, I can't make decisions like that. I rarely made snap decisions and I wasn't about to do so now. I knew I needed to take time to think things through and look at the options before I could make any form of commitment. The hardest part was calming my mind long enough to actually think.

Chapter 9

Decision Time!

I'm strong minded and stubborn, I know that! Some might even say I have strong opinions. But sometimes life does that to people. When adversity rears its ugly head some crumble while others dig in for the long haul. But giving in? No, quitting wasn't my way. I wouldn't have got through those early years of abuse if I hadn't been an optimist. I had all my life believed that even if life feels like crap it could get better and I wasn't about to change my philosophy now.

I'm a Pisces. But I'm not the typical Pisces. Sure, I'm sensitive, some would say overly so. Although I'm caring and nurturing I don't have the addictive nature that can apparently derail many Pisces. But my passionate, strong willed, strong minded unforgiving Scorpio moon is ever present. I'm no shrinking violet; I'd learned long ago that when shit happens if you don't look out for yourself, you'll go down with the ship. I knew it was this strong will and enduring optimism that would keep me on the positive path right now.

Over the years I've seen enough research to convince me that chemotherapy and radiation therapy was not for me. I'd proclaimed on numerous occasions that I wouldn't have these therapies and now here I was being told I might be a candidate for both. Here was the true test of my convictions! For me there was no option but one; I was taking the alternative route. The hardest part would be telling my doctor and the surgeon.

When confronted with situations like this a person very often has cause to reflect on the life they have lived and the inevitable results of their experiences and decisions along the way. I'm the first to admit that I had at times made life more complicated and difficult than it needed to be, mainly because I didn't believe in myself and my own wisdom. Would the journey I was choosing now cause me to regret my decision to ignore the traditional path? Would I be making life more complicated and difficult? Through my ongoing spiritual journey, I've come to realise that life itself is not actually as hard as we think, it is more that we let those uncomfortable human emotions cloud the experience. Once we learn to accept, rather than resist those emotions, life can become easier. Maybe now was the time to truly test this hypothesis.

As the months dragged on, there were times when I felt trapped in a long drawn out fog. I'd chosen a route that until now I had no real knowledge of. I'd elected to use Cansema, a black salve, a natural cancer remedy thousands of years old which when put on the site of a cancer would attack and destroy the cancerous cells. When I made the decision to use Cansema my knowledge was minimal.

I'd read a book written by a cancer survivor and watched the DVD 'One Answer to Cancer' produced by Elaine Hollingsworth. After extensive research, I found it was in common use for skin cancer and melanoma, and many breast cancer sufferers, including a friend of mine, had found success. Surprisingly, I learned that many people knew a great deal about it and its use was widespread. Just the mention of this black salve would invariably elicit the story of someone's experience of successfully using it.

I can't really say why I chose this particular alternative form of treatment other than wanting to avoid the other traditional treatments. It required a great deal of faith that this lonely path I had chosen to heal was made with the right motivation. My faith was unwavering. Surely, this way was preferable to the uncertain outcome the surgeon had outlined. That's not to say I wasn't afraid, I was sick with the fear of the unknown. In my mind, I knew if I chose this path I would have to follow through. It was not a decision to make lightly but I hoped and prayed I was making the right one. At least I was going to give it a shot. If it failed at least I'd know I tried.

Of course, my GP, and especially the breast surgeon considered my decision radical, and foolish. I understood their concerns; I sincerely appreciated their follow up phone calls asking if I'd studied the relevant research literature. Had I thought this though? Had I made a careful and rational consideration? I knew this must have been especially baffling for them, aware as they were, that I had been a volunteer in the Cancer Council WIGS program for a number of years.

However, while volunteering, I'd seen the sadness and fear on the faces of these sick women and it wasn't something I wanted to experience. Volunteering had only cemented my conviction that cutting, poisoning and burning my body could not be the first route I chose for myself. I've never judged others for the health choices they make, and I respect and acknowledge the great number of cancer patients who've been healed through traditional methods. And I wasn't looking for an easy path out of a serious situation. I was well aware of what lay ahead – I'd been pre-warned I'd need some seriously effective pain medication if I took this route.

The thought of such pain was certainly daunting. However, I determined to do what was needed to get through it; I'd give it my best shot even if, in the end it wasn't successful. At least I'd know I'd tried. *After all,* I thought, *you don't get to my age without experiencing some pain along the way.* I'd had three babies and had experienced the body ripping pain that had brought me to my knees. I'd suffered sinusitis accompanied by a pain so intense it was akin to being smashed in the face with a brick. And the years of intense migraines when I lay in bed for days pulling at my hair and praying for it to end. And the foot surgeries for Mortens Neuroma and the ongoing painful healing process of my arthritic toe fusion. Yes, I knew this was going to be different; this was something that had no definitive time limit and I knew once committed there was no turning back.

Although I had confidence in my decision, I was well aware that under these stressful circumstances my body would need support and other forms of nourishment and care. I knew my naturopath, well regarded in her field and having lectured in natural medicine, was the one person who would know what my body needed, someone who could support me throughout this journey.

Being someone with a positive attitude, someone who rarely asked for help, it was a challenging experience to accept that I would need help to do this properly. Since retiring, Ron had always spent much of his time researching and planning his three or four holidays each year, visiting far off islands and countries in Asia. He's a sun lover who says, 'The hotter the better.' When the winter temperature at home is 8°C for three days in a row he says, 'I'm out of here.' Winter for him is misery, so come June he's usually off to warmer weather. For Ron, my cancer diagnosis in early June meant a cold winter at home. I'm so grateful that he was there when I'd needed him.

'I'm here for the long-haul, honey' he'd said, 'I'm here for as long as it takes.'

We made regular trips to the naturopath in Brisbane to monitor my progress and to get the natural health supplements. Ron was wonderfully supportive, whenever my confidence looked to falter he would be there cheering me on.

To some people it may seem foolish that I chose to tackle my breast cancer this way. Sure, I wanted to avoid surgery and the traditionally accepted therapies and had chosen not to have the chemotherapy and radiation therapy that brought people to a standstill. However, cancer always takes a part of you whatever course of action you might embark on. Out of nowhere the plans you've made have to be cancelled or put on hold for who knows how long.

The treatment, whatever method you choose depletes your energy. You lose days and weeks where all you can do, or want to do, is rest. My body was going through a great deal of trauma in its own way; there were days where I felt so wiped out, I would just want to lie on the bed for hours either dozing of just looking into space. I was wearied in body and spirit. My mind wanted to do so much but I was forced to accept that my body was processing the experience and I needed to let go of the guilt of doing nothing. And perhaps it was now time to let the secrets out, and to let others in!

Chapter 10

How Do I Tell My Children?

Telling your family about health concerns is always the dilemma isn't it? I'd fortunately pre-warned Petah about the biopsy so when I rang her the day I received my test results, something I wouldn't normally do, she guessed immediately that it wasn't good news. Her reaction was as I expected; supportive and in control of her emotions. I felt grateful for her calmness, but I still had to tell my two boys. Craig lived 1500 kilometres away in New South Wales and Adam lived three hours away on the Gold Coast and I naturally didn't want them to worry.

'Petah' I said, 'how do I ring the boys and tell them? Do I say, hi how are you going? Oh, by the way I have breast cancer. How do I do that just out of the blue?'

Petah, ever the beautiful, supportive, caring go between said, 'Don't worry Mum, I'll tell the boys, it's better if I do it anyway.'

I know the universe has a way of giving us what we need. All my life I'd wanted to be a mother, to have children to love in a way I had never felt loved. Studies and research conducted on children who've been abused or adopted has shown this to be a common feeling among this group. My biggest fear had always been the possibility of having a daughter; terrified she'd be subjected to the same sexual abuse as me. Unknown to Petah, I therefore spent all her formative years being hyper-vigilant, making sure she was safe. How blessed was I to be gifted with such a beautiful caring and thoughtful daughter? A daughter is a gift to be nurtured. I know, without a shadow of doubt, that a higher power had known best what I needed.

Of course, hearing your mother has cancer is something no child expects to hear. The thought is simply too hard to contemplate. I wasn't sure how my boys would feel or how they'd process the news. Were they shocked? Apparently so! Were they afraid for me or for themselves, worried I'd not be able to win this fight? I hoped not. As usual I made light of it all and told them I was considering alternative therapies. My beautiful sons, both amazing young men were in full support of my choices.

Craig and his wife Tatjana are alternative thinkers in areas of health and wellbeing so my decision was something they never questioned. To them it made sense to keep the poisons out of my body. Craig also spoke of other forms of therapy he'd recently researched. In the odd moment where I felt at a loss and confused, I dearly wished he was here with me. Perhaps there were other ways to heal that would've had quicker less painful results, but I was too overwhelmed. I was in a state of fog where I couldn't think outside my own fear. I felt totally at sea. Just to have had my family close by, to offer a listening ear, would have been such a comfort.

However, I was determined to stay positive both for myself and for my family. I often wondered over the ensuing months whether I was simply in denial over the whole affair or if I was in fact coping well. I'd had a few small 'pity me' weeping sessions in the early stages of treatment but I had never felt a need to completely 'let go.' No doubt being supervised by my naturopath helped me keep focused on the whole of body wellness rather than simply targeting the cancer itself.

Giving in was not an option I assured Adam when we spoke about it later. He was my baby after all; isn't that what many of us call our youngest. I felt I had to tell him that he needn't worry about me succumbing to this scourge.

'Don't worry I'm not going to die Adam, I'm staying strong and I'll beat this,' I stated bravely. I know I tried to sound brave although I'm sure he heard the quiver in my voice.

'I know you will Mum, you're the strongest person I know.'

It was hard trying to sound positive and it made me feel stronger once I heard Adam's words. I was okay while I didn't talk about the cancer. It was only when I actually got into a conversation that the reality hit home, and I felt vulnerable. During the conversations I had with my children and a few other family members of mine and Ron's, and a small group of close friends, I made it clear I didn't want to dwell on the fact I was dealing with cancer and I definitely did not want sympathy. I was adamant I didn't want to talk about it. Taking about it made it too real – and retelling the story over and over got boring after a while.

'I'm not sick and there's no reason to act like I am,' I'd state firmly. And I wasn't sick, that was the absurdity of it all.

Yes, there were many times when I wished my family lived closer to me. My logical mind would tell me my children had busy lives and commitments they just couldn't walk away from to be with me. That however didn't stop the emotional and overly sensitive human part of me feeling a little neglected.

I marvel at what funny, contradictory, mere mortals humans are, especially me! I'd told everyone that I didn't want any special attention, that I just wanted to get on with living as normal a life as I could under these circumstances, hadn't I? No dramas about what might or might not happen. Why then, did I feel this sense of abandonment? I've played the ultra-strong independent, can do anything kind of woman, forever, and now people just accepted I was doing okay. But what if I needed to draw on their strength, just a little? Were they afraid I'll fall apart? Perhaps I will, I'd think dejectedly, after all, I haven't really cried much at all. That is, really cried, that desperate emotion releasing heart-wrenching cry.

In the beginning, as I sat, as I often did, on my patio looking out across my lush garden I wondered if I needed to cry. But, I didn't know how to cry. Maybe I really was in denial. Strong people don't cry they just get on with what they need to do. Maybe I don't cry because I grew up in an era where parents told their children if they cried, they'd be given something to really cry about. This was doubly so with my father. At the first sign of a tear I'd suck it back in and deal with it internally. Crying doesn't really solve anything anyway, it just makes my eyes all puffy, I'd think with amusement.

However, it was during these alone times that I'd feel that small element of doubt creep into my thoughts. Have I done the right thing in choosing this path to heal? Am I not in touch with reality? Fortunately, these negative thoughts didn't occupy my mind for too long and I could dismiss them when I thought of the alternative route I'd been advised to take. I'm human after all, surely, it's normal to feel a little lost at times; isn't it?

Chapter 11

Getting On With Getting On

During this long process I had reason to wonder, *Am I too secretive? Am I too concerned with keeping information about myself private? I'm damned if I know!* Secrecy was the barricade I hid behind, growing up as I did always in fear of being found out. Often, now, as I lay on my bed trying not to dwell on the pain, I'd ask myself why I couldn't let it go. So, at such times I found the best medicine was to just lie as still as possible and go with the flow and try not to analyse the why of it. But, the downside was that it gave free rein to my overactive imagination.

I was finally beginning to realise it was not always to my advantage to portray myself as the strong independent woman. Why then do I cling to privacy so adamantly when it means people don't know when I need them? Could it be because I've always considered sickness in myself a weakness? I sure as hell did not want to be seen as weak! No matter what, I have always managed to work through the sickness and pain trying not to draw undue attention to myself. Was this my subconscious mind attempting to counteract what I'd witnessed for most of my life with Mum? Observing her unconsciously using sickness as a way of gaining attention or perhaps it was a cry for love – and then in later years overmedicated, with one medication counteracting the other.

And why was I revisiting these negatives of the past, now? Surely, I had my own healing to do! Perhaps it was my situation and too much idle time on my hands. My own mortality was at stake – the past was behind me and I had many more fruitful years ahead. I was full of gratitude for the strength

I had been able to tap in to – to move on and grow in wisdom – to let go of what no longer served me. I was reminded of the guilt and disappointment Mum was unable to erase from her mind even in her later years. Unlike me she had been denied the chance of bearing children and it was something that she could never come to terms with.

Dad's abuse of me was something Mum never outwardly acknowledgment to me but I know that cruel twist of fate significantly affected her. While she never understood or acknowledged the psychological impact the abuse had had on me, her own psychological wellbeing suffered. I believe the guilt ate at her soul. No amount to medication was able to erase her shame at the part she played in it; thus, she became a bitter self-centered woman in old age, to me at least.

Was this a lesson for me to take in? To acknowledge the good fortune that had come my way. Sure, there were many years where I struggled to find my place in the world, and now this cursed cancer, but perhaps Mum was right all along. Maybe I hadn't been hurt – I had achieved all I had dreamed of – I was okay! And perhaps, in truth, it wasn't so much that she resented me, maybe it was actually that I did what she never could do – bear children. And the ignominy of it was that with it came the shame of me being an unwed mother.

During my cancer recuperation I had a lot of time to reflect, to look back and review my life's journey. Fortunately, I have few regrets as I've endeavoured to not dwell too much on what has happened in the past, especially the negatives. Instead I've tried my best to be as good a person as I could be with the knowledge I had. However, I have two regrets. One, that I never had the courage to fully open up and address my feelings and thoughts about Mum's earlier neglect and later her psychological torment. The second, that I was not emotionally or psychologically strong enough to report my father and see him punished for his crime. They say that time heals and for me it was my parents passing that allowed me to put that part of my past life to rest. Strange as it may seem although Dad was the abuser, Mum was the one I was most disappointed in. Hers was the love I desperately sought and needed and could never gain.

You might be wondering why I haven't mentioned Mum and Dad's passing. My last vision of Mum was of her lying in the hospital bed, with a tube in her arm, waiting for her final curtain call. I stood at her bedside looking down at her stillness, she, looking up at me, unable to speak. Somehow, I felt she knew what I was saying when I spoke my last words to her, 'Mum, why didn't you love me?' I believe she understood as her eyes were focused on me while I spoke; and of course, she had already given me her answer. Later, there was a part of me that felt ashamed; *Had I become so cynical that I was unable to give her a peaceful exit from her own life of disappointment and hurt?*

Ironically, my last interaction with Dad was that same day, in the same hospital, four rooms up from Mum's. I had no intention of seeing or speaking to him, but the nursing staff had been continually pestering me and Wayne for four days, appealing for us to visit him. Against my own better judgment, I finally relented and regretted it immediately. There was no pleasant or joyful greeting on his part as one might expect after such a long estrangement. His first response at seeing me was 'I'm dying, I have cancer.' I really didn't care!

The major content of his monologue – no he didn't ask after me or mine – was how he planned on his death, to give his car to his friend's daughter – the one in the caravan park I mentioned elsewhere – and how he'd be distributing his possessions. There was no mention of Wayne or me in this. It actually brought back the memories of the multitude of times, when he was badgering and abusing me, his intended enticement, the promise to leave everything he had to me (which I never believed, the liar that he was) because Mum had planned to leave her house to Wayne. Which of course she did.

That was my last visit to each of them – I flew to Cairns to attend Craig's first wedding a few days later. Mum passed away in late June while I was gone; I wasn't there for her funeral which only Wayne and Mum's neighbour attended. A year or so later Wayne received information to say Dad had passed away too. Neither he nor I had been notified at the time, so we have no idea what actually transpired, or when. I actually think we were kept from knowing until it was too late to lay claim to his possessions.

But, to be honest, we cared not a jot for anything he had as it was what we had expected from him anyhow.

Perhaps I sound heartless but now I'd finally realised I no longer needed to feel guilty, the ties were broken, I could get on with life; worrying what others thought of me was too exhausting. I understood the importance of valuing the relationships I now had, valuing the people who had always been there for me, offering support when I needed it most. The same people who were supporting me now through my cancer journey.

My reflections took on a different aspect now too. In the past I have often judged others on my own intrinsic history rather than on their person. I'm now more compassionate, more able to see that everyone walks their own path – in their own time – in their own way.

Chapter 12

My Healing Journey

The winter months passed slowly, followed by the fresh air of spring bringing with it the warmth of the sun. It's amazing how sunshine can have the ability to lift one's spirits, allowing positive thoughts to surface and the body to bask in the suns healing energy. I knew I still had a long way to go. Cancer is a lonely journey without loved ones by your side. I began to feel a need to reconnect with the outside world again after hibernating during the colder months, in a healing mode. I needed my spirits' and morale boosted and I dearly wished my family could be here by my side, bringing me comfort.

During the cancer journey, it always amused me when those in the know would comment with surprise and wonder at how well I looked. *After all*, I'd think to myself, *I have cancer and I'm not supposed to look well; How lucky am I?* Because I'd avoided the ravages of chemotherapy and radiation, I looked quite normal. But there were cracks in the armour I had surrounded myself with. I hid it very well and in hindsight I can see that it may not have been in my best interest to be so private about my health issue. In reality, until you have cancer you can't really have a true understanding of what it is or how it affects you. There is an unreality about it and you need to experience it to truly understand how frightening it can be.

From time to time, during the black salve journey, I recorded some of my thoughts and feelings in a personal journal. On Monday 21 November 2016, the entry recorded the following:

Five and a half months have passed and there is no clear end in sight. Last night was a sleepless one; I finally fell into bed at 4.15am and it took a further 20 minutes before I finally nodded off. My black salve wound started giving me grief earlier in the evening and I've finally had to succumb to taking pain medication. I'd stubbornly held off taking anything for the pain until it was really beyond my ability to think myself out of it. Today was dressing day and just going through the process was excruciating.

I'm tired, so tired. So, my pain threshold is at a low ebb. I'm definitely feeling sorry for myself and probably a smidgen irrational. As the tears roll down my cheeks feelings of abandonment and loss rise to the surface and I've begun to feel angry and sad. It's times like this, when my body is low in energy and depleted of natural health and vitality, that it's so easy to overreact and theorise about everything.

My mind is working overtime on all the negative scenarios imaginable. Poor sad me! Nearly six months have passed and in all that time where have my sons been? Who, apart from Petah, and my dearest friend Sue, has come to visit and see how I am really travelling? Who really cares about my wellbeing? This is the first time any of the kids have been touched by a loved one's cancer. I thought they'd be more concerned.

Thoughts continued to flow as do my tears. What have I failed to teach them? I keep telling myself that always being the strong mother, who rarely asked for help, had done neither me nor them any favours. My best friend has shown more caring and compassion than my children have. She had flown down from Townsville twice to check on my progress and made weekly and sometimes twice weekly phone calls.

Sadly, I know that as we age, we have to come to terms with and accept that once our children grow up and move away to develop families of their own, they lose a significant link to their primary family. I of all people, should know that. After all I have studied development psychology and sociology as part of my Psychology Degree. But I am human after all! Also, within me, there is that ever present and deep-seated subconscious sense of not being worthy – am

I loved? That ever-present push/pull! I'm strong and I don't need your pity or sympathy – but I'm afraid and I need you to show me I'm cared about! Such a contradiction!

I understand Craig lives 1500 kilometres away in New South Wales. He's busy building his own home and engaged in family matters. He's taken time off from full employment to complete the house build, he can't drop everything and visit me even if he wanted to. He telephones occasionally but I always tell him I'm doing well. He has no reason to doubt me. He respects me for my chosen treatment option. Adam is 250 kilometres away at the Gold Coast. It's unfortunate that I have only been able to see him once in these six months. I try not to feel and think negatively about this because, like Craig, he has family responsibilities and financial restraints which prevent him from just dropping everything. But unlike Craig, and due to his ocular albinism, Adam doesn't have the ability to jump in a car and come to visit.

Of course, I have no doubt that my children love me, I'm sure of it. There are many others too who care a great deal about me. However, I've been forced to reflect on the significance and meaning of that love. My thoughts bring me to realise that it is not so much that I doubt their love for me, it is more about my inner loneliness, my need for their need of me. They no longer require my nurturing and I've been left feeling redundant. However, these misery thoughts are transient and do not linger long. My rational and logical mind accepts that I need to give an outlet to my honest feelings, meanwhile my inner soul silently yearns for more.

During this time, I had reason to reflect on my relationship with my own mother, wondering if in some way I could have been a better daughter. I know during my primary years I loved her so very much. However, I accept now that my love for her wasn't enough; she was unable to reciprocate the love I so badly needed. I know because of this I grew up promising myself that when I had children, I would love them unconditionally. I would show them in every way I could that they were the centre of my world. Along the way I've made many mistakes as a parent, some even cringe worthy. But I've learned that life is a school and we parents are all here as students too.

I've tried not to dwell on what mistakes I've made. There's no use feeling guilty at not being a perfect person and a perfect daughter. Rightly or wrongly I long ago set about creating the life I wanted in the future. Through the help of therapy, I realised my task was to simply live a life true to myself, and to forgive myself for the mistakes I've made. I know now that I can't take responsibility for other's opinions, or their expectations, or their perceived hurts caused by me. I am who I am, and I must continue to attempt to live as honest a life as I can, being the best version of myself I can be.

Chapter 13

A Cruel Twist Of Fate

I'd love to say that my alternative journey was a roaring success but unfortunately it wasn't. After six months of keeping a positive outlook, experiencing a great deal of pain, my alternative route failed to achieve the results I'd hoped for. The cancer was too deep seated – I was forced to concede defeat. My follow-up ultrasound clearly indicated the growth in my breast had not diminished and could have in fact grown. Once again, with a sinking heart, I was forced to reconsider the more traditional methods of treatment.

This time the journey took on a different look. Because I had felt underwhelmed at our initial surgeon consultation, I decided to consult another oncologist, one who was highly recommended by many professionals, and who was also a reconstructive surgeon. Ron and I were immediately impressed by her enthusiastic and positive outlook. She explained in great detail the many options available, thus we left feeling less uncertain of the road ahead. Of course, the ensuing journey proposed, a bilateral mastectomy and reconstruction, was daunting. I was by no means looking forward to the months ahead, but I was no longer in a position to bargain with my own life.

Of course, there was a multitude of tests to be done before hand, such as an MRI, Bone Scan, and Ultrasounds. Due to my constant back pain in the thoracic area, the x-rays were also done to ensure there was no secondary cancer in the vertebrae. With each test, there was always that uneasy feeling – might there be something else going on that I didn't know about. During our few consultations, I made it very clear I didn't want, and would not have, chemotherapy or radiation therapy. Fortunately, I have been blessed with good general health. I have no other ailments other than some joint problems and I made it clear I didn't want to poison my immune system with such poisons. I was grateful when I was diagnosed with positive hormonal type of cancer which meant I was able to take a tablet which would ensure further cancer was kept at bay.

While I was dreading the surgery, I none the less wanted, now that the decision was made, to get it over with as soon as possible. I needed to put this whole sorry episode behind me, for once and for all. But, as the surgery appointment date approached, with only a few weeks to go, I suddenly began having extreme headaches, sensations akin to a knife being driven through the top of my skull and in behind my eye. There was also a slight rash developing on my forehead and over the bridge of my nose which I thought might be due to stress. And, as one might imagine, my first thought was, *Do I have secondary brain cancer?* Luckily, I had an appointment for acupuncture with my GP a few days later. After describing my symptoms and sharing my worries, I asked could it be brain cancer? As quick as a flash, after a bit of a scratch through the blisters on my head, she diagnosed shingles.

What a twist of fate this was! I was both relieved that it wasn't serious, and disappointed because it was another thing I had to contend with. Luckily, because I was diagnosed within the three-day period, I was prescribed a week of medication which halted the shingles in its tracks and preventing it from developing further. I guess by now I should have been accustomed to pain, but this was another level again, but at least my worst fears had been allayed. My concern now was, *Would I be well again by the surgery date?* Everything takes time and patience and fortunately I was back on track and the surgery went ahead.

Fortunately, the three-and-a-half-hour surgery was successful and after five sleepless nights in hospital, I went home to my own bed. Because I had elected to have reconstruction surgery, I'd been fitted with breast expanders in readiness for the later reconstruction surgery. For the next ten days, I had drainage tubes attached to my body which were tricky to manoeuvre. Time seems to go slowly when you lose your independence, when you have to rely on others for sustenance and transport. While he might have let me starve, (he doesn't cook), I was grateful for Ron's unwavering support through this whole long process.

Life can get back to normal fairly quickly when you are well. I had been living a very healthy and sugarless diet for nine months and I'm sure this went a long way toward my healing process. Because my lymph nodes were clear of cancer, I avoided the argument I didn't want to have, regarding the dreaded radiation therapy. Fortunately, my resolve wasn't tested. As with most surgery, the recovery was painful, and I needed strong pain medication for a few weeks. My body was depleted of energy and I needed a lot of rest. However, I do not want to belabour this as I feel eternally grateful for having come through it all so well.

My reconstruction surgery was not as intense as the initial mastectomy surgery and I was only required to stay in hospital for two nights. Of course, it was many weeks of healing after the reconstruction surgery before I felt the process was behind me and I was now able to get on with a normal life once more. The journey had been a long one and at times a frustratingly pain filled one. Although the alternative process I undertook was unsuccessful I have no regrets and in fact feel deep gratitude for the experience. The further journey along the traditional route taught me many things about life and about the people around me. I actually began to realise how many people do care about me and love me. Perhaps there might have been more if I had let them know what I was experiencing. I know that the fourteen months of pain and uncertainty are all a part of the life I chose to embark upon this time round.

Chapter 14

A Spiritual Quest

I'm not a religious person, that is I don't belong to a particular religious denomination. Not that I haven't tried over the years to find a church community where I could gain a sense of belonging, where I could find family and peace. My first religious experience was attending Sunday school as a young child and I retain many beautiful memories of that time where I joyfully absorbed the bible stories. There was always the pleasure of bringing home the small cards covered with lovely images of bible characters and small bible verses on them. Unfortunately, this all ceased when we began our itinerant lifestyle.

I was during my late thirties that I set out on a religious or spiritual quest. Over the years I've sought solace from many different religious denominations but sadly each time I've been disappointed and discouraged. The problem was that religion failed to provide me with the reassurance and self-confidence I needed. Perhaps I was seeking the love that I was longing for, a verification of my worthiness and deservedness of love.

I believe in God and Jesus, that God is loving, kind and forgiving. I believe too that God is often sad and disappointed in many of the decisions we make and the actions we take, but I don't believe he judges us. This I believe is something he leaves to us when our earthly life ceases. He gives us the opportunity to review our life and reflect on our character and actions and see where we could have done better.

Because I believe that God is a God of love, I found it disappointing and saddening to hear from the ministers of many religious denominations how worthless and sinful we mere mortals are. And how we, such unworthy creatures, are born in sin. I admit I have sinned, sometimes unknowingly, sometimes under pressure, and at other times knowing full well what I was doing. For someone like me, someone who desperately needed to feel worthy and loved, this form of ministering only resulted in me feeling more shame and guilt. I would almost always come away from the church service feeling sad and tearful, more lost than ever.

Try as I might I could never find the peace I sought by attending a church service. This seems such a contradiction to me now; when I think about the joy I feel when I travel abroad and spend hours wandering through historical cathedrals and churches in many of the European cities. It is at such times, when I enter the peaceful and calming environment, that I can appreciate the quiet solace within the church. I can understand how multitudes of people over millennia have continued to worship in these havens of tranquility, finding comfort and peace for their souls.

Blake D. Bauer in his book, *You Were Not Meant to Suffer*, writes that in today's world of spiritual and holistic way of seeing things it is widely accepted that most forms of cancer in the human body has its origin in repressed psychological and emotional anger. Internalising, denying and repressing what we feel, think, want or need out of fear is unhealthy and self-destructive. He contends that at the centre of our unhealthy pattern of internalising, denying and repressing what we feel and think, is the fact that many of us never felt safe or supported enough growing up to fully express ourselves.

I can now see, on a deeper level, that I had never learned to be present to my inner world or verbalised what I truly felt, thought, desired or needed at any time throughout my entire childhood and adolescent years. I compromised, abandoned and betrayed myself as a young child thus I began to repress, deny and internalise my thoughts and feelings because I feared the pain I associated with losing the love, acceptance, approval and support of my parents. I can see clearly that I wanted so badly to be loved by my mother that I denied a part of my own personhood until the day she died. It's unfortunate that in those early years when I did muster the strength and courage to express myself in the best way I knew how I was met with either anger and abuse or indifference and disregard.

Dealing with deep emotional pain has demands on a person. In a strange way while I was present in pain fully, I was also in some way an observer from a distance, almost as thought I was watching a movie. In hindsight, it is easy to see why I developed a pattern of internalising my thoughts, feelings, desires, needs, and dreams because it didn't seem to matter to anyone whether I spoke about them of not. Consequently, I gave up trying to express myself. My heart was hurting, and I never learned to consciously express how I felt. On the outside, the side I presented to the world, I was the outgoing friendly, confident, outspoken person; on the inside I was self-critical, lacking in confidence, and wondering what my purpose was in being here.

For quite some time I did harbour anger and resentment for the past pain I experienced. However, I haven't consciously placed blame on others or certain circumstances for the life I have ultimately created for myself. Over time I've learned, after many trials and tribulations, that ultimately, I needed to accept responsibility for my life in its entirety if I was to live a full and purposeful life. Feeling or acting a victim would not benefit me at all. Growing up as I did, I learned that a 'poor me' attitude would not stop the bad stuff happening. Yes, I was a victim of sexual, psychological and emotional abuse but I had to learn to rise above the blame game and look for the life purpose behind the circumstances of my life and begin to honour the strength I was gifted to endure it.

My quest has taught me that life is about choices; I had to accept responsibility for my own life and the choices I ultimately made. I knew what I wanted from life and made every attempt to achieve it. I've searched for answers to my many questions over the years and agree with John Shipp when he says, 'You either get better or you get bitter. It's that simple. You either take what has been dealt to you and allow it to make you a better person or you allow it to tear you down. The choice does not belong to fate it belongs to you.'

Chapter 15

Trust And Love

The psychological impact of those early years was deep seated and it was many years before I recognised the impact this had had on my life. During those early years I'd felt lost and confused – how had no one seen this? I've wondered, *Would things have been different if I had acted sad and miserable, or angry and spiteful? Would anyone have questioned why I acted that way? Would my mother have felt empathy for me if she had acknowledged the abuse was happening?*

No! She actually seemed to resent my being able to get on with life, to act like a normal person and not dwell on the bad experiences. Because I was able to conceal my confused mental state, she had no comprehension or interest in what damage had been done to my psyche. I'd become too good an actress and thus I was fair fodder for her ongoing derision.

On too many occasions, when I had broached the subject of my troubled state of mind, she'd redirected the conversation to her own issues—no doubt guilt or regret—for which she had been seeing a psychologist. It seemed that she could not or would not see beyond my ability to get on with life. I see now that her guilt must have been immense, a heavy burden to admit her part in my abuse, thus she had to redirect her guilt on to me by stating, 'All these years I've worried that you were harmed. But you're married and have three beautiful children and you have lots of friends, there is nothing wrong with you.'

Because she couldn't see the scars, she didn't believe I had been harmed. Even when I cried and said, 'Mum, you can't see inside my head, you don't know what I feel inside.'

She simply could not, would not, acknowledge to me at least, the part she had played in the sad scenario. I'd had to cover up the abuse for so long even I didn't know who I really was, or how I was supposed to feel and act. It had just become second nature for me to hide that secret traumatised self from her and the world. Outwardly, I portrayed a vibrant and happy persona; I was able to socialise and interact with the world without disclosing a minuscule of information about myself. I was a closed book; I'd learned to hold back trust, especially in the areas of friendship and love. And the secret had to be kept at all cost.

And, there was that deep-seated feeling of being unlovable. After all, hadn't Dad always told me that I wasn't good looking, that he was the only one who would love me. But I'd learned early on that love was not good; it's abuse, and a loss of power over your life. How then could I tell when someone really felt genuine love for me? Where was the real me in all of this? How does one learn to let go of that ingrained sense of worthlessness?

As I read David D. Bauer's words in his book, *You Were Not Meant to Suffer*, I realised the wisdom he spoke; that we need to realise the people who birthed us or raised us could not give us what they hadn't been given or learned for themselves. If they were unable to accept and love themselves entirely then it makes sense that they were unable to relate to us in a loving and kind way, even if they wanted and tried to.

There were times during my formative years, though more so through the middle age years, when I have wondered if I was capable of feeling love. Did I have the capacity to feel unconditional love? Why was I always holding back, not allowing myself to feel fully engaged— never letting go— never allowing myself to be vulnerable to another being? How could I say 'I love you' when I didn't know what it was supposed to feel like, what it really meant? Perhaps it was because I'd learned through the many years of powerlessness and fear that if you accept love, there will be a payback, there would always be a price to pay.

I have tried over the years to analyse this – wondering if it is my nature to be unable to trust. Or was it the ongoing abuse I'd endured that had caused me to feel disconnected and different. I experienced a number of relationships during my early twenties where I connected on some level but it was only in hindsight that I realised it was more about seeking another's love and admiration than giving it. By gaining this admiration and love was I perhaps trying to convince myself I really was loveable?

There was always that push/pull feeling within me. For many years after being freed from the stranglehold of abuse, I was unaware how the distress and fear caused by Dad's controlling abuse had impacted my ongoing interaction in the world. Deep within there was that feeling of not being worthy – I was unable to use my own power. For a long time, I was afraid of anger, of hearing something negative about myself which would further deepen my self-depreciation, so I avoided confrontation.

Whatever the reason behind my past feelings and thoughts regarding my selfhood I sometimes felt a powerlessness that prevented me from refusing a sexual request. Would I be rejected, and left feeling even more unloved? That ingrained subconscious fear of the repercussions of refusing, followed by the ultimate disappointment and self-shame, was a constant battle within me. For fifteen years I had been abused and betrayed by my father in the name of love, how could I possibly know if the love someone professed for me was real.

I didn't believe I could receive genuine love, especially from men. And I didn't know if I could feel it either. Sure, I had the odd feeling of wanting it from others but because I didn't truly understand what love is, there was always that reserve. 'I love you' were words I could never say. Always that underlying fear that if I let someone see my vulnerability I would not be able to withdraw from it – there would always be a price to pay. Like many others, I'm still a work in progress.

As I matured, I began to look for the reasons, apart from my family dynamics, underlying my lack of self-love and self-esteem. As more knowledge of my true history unfolded in later years I realised that much of this was tied up with my feelings of abandonment and the relinquishment by my birth mother for adoption. My sense of betrayal ran deep and this, added to the sexual abuse, underscored all the feelings I had about myself. What kind of mother could give her baby away? And to people like these? To be abused and taken advantage of so badly – to not feel loved and cared for. To not have a voice, a choice. The sweet words that were bandied around about how being adopted was so wonderful because you were a chosen one, were, to me, lies.

Was I so unlovable at eighteen months that I wasn't worth keeping? These thoughts were replayed over and over in my mind and as the abuse continued, and the years rolled on, my resentment grew toward my birth mother and adoptive parents. My knowledge of my adoption was another secret I was forced to keep, first from my mother, then from the rest of the world. I felt that my life was just one huge lie.

It's gratifying to see that over the past decades the public's awareness, education and perception of adoption has changed. In the past adoption was never discussed with many children never being informed of their birth history. To be born out of wedlock, was to be a bastard, a cause of deep shame and embarrassment for the mother and her family. Girls who'd had a baby out of wedlock could never expect to be wanted or respected by another man. No one would be foolish enough to disclose their true parentage for fear of judgment. This was just one more thing that I feared would be my undoing if found out. Then to be an unwed mother myself compounded my sense of judgment – who was I to judge the decisions of those who had gone before me. It felt to me that my whole life was a series of lies, of covering up the truth of who I really was. Just who then was I?

Chapter 16

Pain And Forgiveness

'When we are no longer able to change a situation we are challenged, then, to change ourselves.' Victor Frankl – *Man's Search for Meaning*.

My continual search for meaning has directed me toward psychiatric therapy and wise counsel over a period of time when I was most troubled. Studying self-help material has also assisted me to understand the meaning of self-love. I agree with Blake D. Bauer when he says in his book, *You Were Not Meant to Suffer*, 'Within us we have the sense of an inner plan directing us forward—propelling us onward in faith.' His wisdom has helped me see that I either wait for a saviour to come along or I tap in to my own innate strength and learn to accept who I am and learn to love myself unconditionally.

A great deal of research has been done in recent years and it seems that love, or lack of love, greatly influences who or what we become. Feeling loved can show us we are worthwhile beings and helps us to foster and develop our ability to share ourselves in healthy ways. It took me a long time to realise that right up until Mum's death, all I yearned for was a sign of her affection and love, a sign that I was worthwhile. Possibly, subconsciously, that was the reason I kept going back. One day she might tell me she loved me.

I, no doubt, was a great actress, perhaps I missed my true calling, as over the years I'd had a lot of practice—I was good at faking a happy façade. However, I wished and prayed that just once Mum would look beyond the façade and see my internal anguish and recognise how much I needed her. Each conversation I attempted, and there were many, she'd brush me aside or cut me off midsentence. I'd tried telling her what was happening to me on many occasions, but she'd quickly change the subject. I truly believe that she knew what was going on—it was simply in her best interest to hide it from herself.

As much as I wanted her attention, sadly even my touch repulsed her. The years of hiding the shame of what was taking place and the constant fear of being found out took its toll. My constant hyper-vigilance and anxiety caused my hands to sweat continuously and this clamminess was what repulsed her. When I would touch her, as children do, she'd draw back, exclaiming, 'Don't touch me, you're like a frog.' She simply could not bear for me to touch her and this never changed, even until her death.

While it took me a long time to forgive Dad and Mum for what I saw as their failings, I now have a clearer understanding of how life's disappointments may have impacted their lives. We never actually know what makes a person who they are, do we? Or what life experiences have caused them to act the way they do. My parents' generation were people who thought children should be seen and not heard. As a result of knowing very little of how they viewed the world—giving little away in respect of what they thought or felt internally, or what pain they harboured within—we hardly knew them.

Many of us hold memories and pain which have, at some time, caused us to feel confused about who we really are. I know, unless you face your own shadows, you will continue to see them in others, because the world outside is only a reflection of the world inside you. Dealing with trauma and overcoming it is a strength we all have. I've learnt through experience you can make a difference in your own world -but you need to work at it - you can't expect others to make changes for you. A Jack London quote I found recently says it well, 'Life is not always a matter of holding good cards, but sometimes, playing poor cards well.'

Chapter 17

Acceptance And Gratitude

My need for reading has never diminished and fortunately, that young girl who used books as an escape has now gone. Nowadays, I've developed a love of reading that empowers me to delve into the inner workings of me as a human. In fact, the countless spiritually based self-help and personal development books I've devoured since those early years have facilitated my healing process, helping to restore my once minimal sense of self-worth and self-confidence.

M Scott Peck, in his book, *The Road Less Travelled*, suggests that our lifetime offers unlimited opportunities for spiritual growth until the end. Spiritual growth, he suggests is the evolution of the individual. He believes this takes effort because of the natural resistance, a natural inclination to keep things the way they were – to take the easy path. He also states that spiritual evolution may seem unrealistic, considering the wars, corruption, and pollution; and because we expect more of ourselves than those that came before us. We grow spiritually through learning to love ourselves then assist others to love themselves.

Fortunately, now my life is more about the journey – and what my experiences have taught me – about how I've perceived those experiences and how they will enhance my future experiences. When I was young, life was about proving and improving myself, about making myself into the person I thought I wanted to be. I set out with nothing but dreams in my mind and was able to accomplish some extraordinary successes. With age, I've learned to be more accepting, to allow and let life unfold. I've learned to have gratitude for the small achievements I've had and the possibility of what may lie ahead. I've learned that while life isn't always fair, no matter how bad a situation may seem, it will change. Life is still good! I'm an 'experiencer.'

Life has become more about doing, choosing because I want to, not because I have to. I have control over most things, except cancer of course; although perhaps this too was a part of my life contract. And yes, I did have control over how I chose to deal with the cancer especially as my first choice of treatment was not the success I envisioned it would be. That experience showed me I oversaw my process, there were other avenues I needed to explore. When things got toughest, I was grateful for the extra strength that helped me pull through.

Reflecting on my birth family I see a history of five children, the youngest only three months old when their father died, being raised by a single mother. I wonder what my life would have been like if I had been a part of it all. I see the divisions and actual dislike some have toward each other and I wonder, *Would I have been inflicted with this feeling toward any of them if I had been there too? Would I have also felt a need to compete for a mother's time and attention?* Sure, I suffered abuse, felt unloved, was under educated and put to work at an early age but I feel in many ways I have been the fortunate one. This is the path my soul chose and I'm okay. I'm not more, or less, than anyone else. I'm just grateful for the strength and resilience I was gifted which helped me through the troubled times, and for the many lessons life has taught me.

My life continues to be a marvelous journey; I've learned that life is meant to be lived, we are not just bystanders looking in. I don't live in regret for anything I've done. I love that I'm still able to dream of what I can and will do in the future. The cancer journey and the couple of other more recent significant surgeries are behind me now. I have so much more to do and see. What I've learned during this eventful adventure is that life doesn't just happen, there has to be some input from us; we have to still dream and work to make these dreams come true.

I've had an amazingly full life! Sure, some of the hurdles were high, but I cleared them. No one is in charge of my happiness but me. I've learned that life is too short to waste time holding on to hate and resentment; all that actually matters at life's end is that you loved. Unfortunately, so many of us lose the ability to dream but I want to encourage you to dream again. All it takes is for you to decide, and then make a commitment, to not give up hope until you achieve your dream.

As Nisargadatta Maharaja says:

There is nothing to practice. To know yourself, be yourself. To be yourself, stop imagining yourself to be this or that. Just be. Let your true nature emerge. Don't disturb your mind with seeking.

Craig's wedding in Denmark, 2008.

My 60th birthday, a small plane flight, 2005.

University Graduation photo, 1996.

Bibliography

Conversations with God, Book 1; An uncommon dialogue, Neale Donald Walsch, Hodder & Stoughton, London, 1996.

Conversations with God, Book 2; An uncommon dialogue, Neale Donald Walsch, Hodder & Stoughton, London, 1997.

Conversations with God, Book 3; An uncommon dialogue. Neale Donald Walsch, Hodder & Stoughton, London, 1998.

The Knight in Rusty Armour. Robert Fisher, Wiltshire Book Company, 1990

The Road Less Travelled; a New Psychology of Love, Traditional Values and Spiritual Growth. M. Scott Beck. Hutchinson & Co. Publishers, Great Britain 1983.

The Slave. Anand Dilvar. Shelter Harbor Press, London, United Kingdom April 2001.

The Subtle Art of Not Giving a F*ck; A counterintuitive approach to living a good life. Mark Manson. HarperOne, New York, 2016.

The Game of Life and How to Play It. Florence Scovel Shinn. DeVorss & Company, California, 1925.

Your Word is Your Wand, Florence Scovel Shinn. DeVorss & Company, California, 1928.

The Secret Door to Success, Florence Scovel Shinn. DeVorss & Company, California, 1928.

The Power of The Spoken Word, Florence Scovel Shinn. DeVorss & Company, California, 1945.

How Are We to Live? Ethics in an age of self-realisation, Peter Singer, The Text Publishing Company, Melbourne Australia, 1993.

Man's Search for Meaning, Victor Frankl, Beacon Press.

You Were Not Meant to Suffer; Love Yourself Back to Inner Peace, Health, Happiness and Fulfillment, Blake D. Bauer, Balboa Press, United States, 2012.

Winnie the Pooh, A. A. Milne, Easton Press, 1926.

CPSIA information can be obtained
at www.ICGtesting.com
Printed in the USA
LVHW010719220620
658653LV00012B/589